Reengineering
Education With Quality

Reengineering Education With Quality

Using Quality Concepts, Techniques, and Tools
to Improve Education

Stanley J. Spanbauer

In Cooperation with Educators in America and Abroad

USA Group Research Institute
PO Box 6180
Indianapolis, Indiana 46206-6180

Reengineering Education With Quality

Stanley J. Spanbauer

Library of Congress Cataloging-in-Publication Data

Spanbauer, Stanley J.
   Reengineering Education With Quality — using quality and productivity concepts, techniques, and tools to improve education; developed by USA Group National Quality Academy in cooperation with educators in America and abroad.
     p. cm.
   Includes bibliographical references (p.) and index.
   ISBN 0-9653351-0-0
   1. Education, United States. 2. Quality Control, United States
LA000.0.000   1996
000.00—0000   00-00000
                                                       CIP

0000000000

ISBN 0-9653351-0-0

Publishing Technician & Cover Design—Don Pavek
Data Entry Technician—Rhonda Kroes
Production Support—Angela Luebke
Production Editor—Cynthia Duerkop
Editor—Jo Hillman

Printed in the United States of America

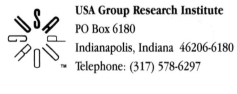

USA Group Research Institute
PO Box 6180
Indianapolis, Indiana 46206-6180
™ Telephone: (317) 578-6297

Table of Contents

List of Illustrations

Acknowledgments

To the instructors, consultants, and other staff of USA Group National Quality Academy. Their enthusiasm for and commitment to excellence is the impetus for innovations which have distinguished the Academy.

To USA Group and Noel-Levitz Centers, Inc., for their support and assistance in establishing, certifying, and maintaining Regional Quality Academies throughout the United States and abroad.

To the Regional Quality Academies, their faculty, and staff who have created living laboratories of TQI in education through their pioneering efforts and creativity.

The dedication and support of educators from these organizations and faculty and staff from other colleges and universities who have become partners with USA Group National Quality Academy has created a synergy to foster meaningful change in education through a focus on continuous improvement.

Foreword

The best way to determine the future is to create it.

Roy A. Nicholson, Chairman and Chief Executive Officer
USA Group, Inc.

No one needs to tell you that these are difficult times in higher education. Financial troubles, shifting student demographics, changing public expectations, and an explosion in information technology are all forcing higher education leadership to look for ways to do better with less. It's not just happening to *someone else*. It's happening at some of the finest institutions in the country.

For centuries, institutions of higher education have demonstrated adaptability and resiliency. Challenges and problems that caused the demise of many businesses have been successfully addressed by colleges and universities. But today, colleges and universities face financial problems that are forcing cutbacks and layoffs in many schools and threaten the very existence of some. Schools of every size, shape, and academic orientation are capping enrollments, limiting courses, reducing salaries, deferring maintenance, curtailing construction, and accelerating the retirement of deans and tenured faculty.

There are significant changes in the public expectations for education. As a result of financial and economic pressures, parents, taxpayers, and lawmakers are demanding more from a nation's colleges and universities—*accountability* is the new watchword. Both the popular press and higher education publications reflect the growing pressure for schools to demonstrate results. Public demands for increased faculty teaching productivity and for documentation of enhanced learning outcomes grow louder. Some say the ivory tower is under siege.

Increased government regulation coupled with reductions in government funding reflect growing concerns about the operations of our institutions. Public support for higher education through the allocation of tax dollars cannot be taken for granted. One thing is clear: the money is not going to be there the way it has been. Governments don't have it. Families don't have it. Scholarship grant funds are becoming increasingly limited. We are going to have to take a harder look at the other side of the equation—at achieving greater cost effectiveness and operating efficiencies. It is no longer *business as usual* on campuses across the nation.

High on the change list for most colleges and universities is generating new resources, lowering costs, and improving services to students. The concept of reengineering offers institutions a way to reinvent the way they do business. Reengineering begins by asking, "If we were to start all over and recreate this business of higher education, how would we do it?" And the key that unlocks the door to reinventing higher education is quality—an abiding preoccupation with quality that provides the tools to create an entirely new way of doing business.

I am happy to report that the reengineering of America's college campuses has already begun. Schools are harnessing quality strategies, information technologies, and new management processes to restructure administrative offices and help students schedule classes, access grades, communicate with professors, and more.

In no small way, these efforts nationally have been championed by Stan Spanbauer, the former college president who made *reengineering education with quality* his personal and institutional vision. After his extraordinary success at Fox Valley Technical College, Stan has made quality his calling. As President of USA Group National Quality Academy, Dr. Spanbauer has shared his vision with hundreds of schools in the U.S. and throughout the world. Realizing that vision without action is always insufficient, he has pioneered dozens of tools—books, courses, and programs—to convert quality principles from theory to campus reality.

That's what this book is all about. Spanbauer showcases eleven institutions that have caught the quality spirit and are well on the way to transforming themselves to better confront the challenges facing us all.

Significant change is in the making for any institution that recognizes both the need and the opportunities for reengineering the way it does business. Together, we must find solutions to assure that this Country's institutions will achieve their missions well into the next century. American higher education is second to none in the world. We rightly take pride in that distinction. We must do everything we can to ensure that this will still hold true in the world our children will inherit.

Preface

Change is sweeping across America. *Made in the USA* is again becoming the symbol of world class quality. America is bouncing back today because people are accepting total quality methods and practices taught to the Japanese decades ago by people like Deming, Juran, and Fiegenbaum. Once again, America is moving forward to regain economic stability. While there is still a ways to go, our businesses and industries are determined to match the *close-to-zero defects* standard set by Japan years ago.

According to the National Association of Manufacturers, in both 1994 and 1995, America was ranked number 1 in the World Competitiveness Report, on a scorecard by the Geneva-based World Economic Forum.[1] What are the reasons for this transformation? Foremost is the realization that today the customer is king and the workplace needs to be more personally fulfilling for employees. The company's success is something employees are proud of. Teams of staff members are running their own internal businesses, in charge of getting orders and supplies, responsible for quality control, shipping, and even the hiring and firing of employees. In America, quality is up, productivity is up, and profits are up.

BUSINESS AND INDUSTRY AFFECTS EDUCATION

This transformation in business and industry dramatically influences public education. Business and government leaders realize that in this knowledge age, a nation's competitive advantage is directly related to how it obtains, compiles, processes, and uses information. Pressure is being applied to educators across America to change the way they do things and to improve their efficiency and effectiveness. Academia is being attacked from all angles. Critics abound and attempts at educational reform are increasing. Most of these reform programs are quick-fix type programs promoted by people external from academia. They focus on cosmetic changes for education. Some suggest alternatives to public education.

One such experiment is occurring in Hartford, Connecticut where the school board is contracted with businesses to run the schools. It all began with great promises. Buildings would be renovated and computer labs installed. Class sizes would be reduced and test scores would go up under a five-year contract between the school district and Education Alternatives, Inc. The entire $200 million budget was turned over in an elaborate privatization effort.

At first it seemed like just the right thing for an ailing educational system. However, a report in the November 13, 1995, issue of *Time* indicates that the plan is not working as predicted. The Hartford School Board is attempting to change the contract because of discontent by both parents and teachers. Similarly, the highly touted Edison Project designed by Christopher Whittle has only four schools in operation, a far cry from the 200 predicted only a few years ago.[2]

Similar failures in Miami Beach and Baltimore have also been highlighted by critics of privatization. The Wall Street Journal on December 6, 1995, reported that Baltimore, the most lucrative contract of Education Alternatives, Inc., has canceled the company's agreement for managing a dozen schools.[3]

In other reform attempts, projects such as *school choice* and *voucher systems* are being advocated as people seek answers to the problems and challenges facing public education. These meager attempts at reform are generally short-term. The reform efforts will continue to have problems because they tend to focus on isolated parts and don't address the entire issue. The efforts are not comprehensive and systematic.

TOTAL QUALITY IMPROVEMENT

There is a way to reform education which will rebuild the system and improve it permanently. This approach shakes the very foundation of the educational system by restructuring the way schools are managed. This approach is sometimes called *Total Quality Management (TQM)*. It is also called *Continuous Process Improvement, Total Quality Leadership,* or *Continuous Quality Improvement*. My preferred title is *Total Quality Improvement (TQI)*. I also like the phrase *educational reengineering*. The terminology used is not important as long as the process involves total commitment to reviewing and reengineering all aspects: administration, student services, and most important, the teaching process, while transforming the culture of the institution.

While many such efforts are postponed by the mistaken belief that better quality costs more, the momentum is growing as more and more schools are deciding it is worth the up-front investment and the risk involved. Today, hundreds of schools around the world are taking the first small, painful steps in quality improvement. Colleges and universities are turning to the principles, techniques, and tools of TQI.

Business schools are revamping their offerings to provide courses and degrees which reflect this new thrust. As they teach these new quality and productivity courses, they begin to realize the importance of *practicing what they preach* by implementing these concepts in their own departments.

Even education administrators are becoming involved. Community executives, lobbying for educators to teach quality management to business and engineering students, are inviting university presidents and school deans to their conferences on quality. As these educational leaders learn more about quality, they look in their own backyards and discover the potential of TQI to rebuild the floundering ships of academia. They begin to implement quality improvement processes in the administrative and service areas of the campus. They soon realize that the classroom itself is logical place for the quality push in education.

This transformation is not easy. There are several hurdles. While a growing number of educators are using TQI as the process to change how they do things, the sheer size of the task of applying quality throughout the education system seems overwhelming to others. It is difficult to engage in quality programs because of tradition and the structure of education. Also, in this era of tight budgets, it is difficult to find the money needed to pave the way.

However, there are some positive signs. Most educators realize that something needs to be done and many believe that TQI may be the answer. While they view the ideas with some suspicion, they know that there is hope because, if TQI is properly applied, internal people begin to champion the cause and drive the change. This preliminary effort by a few champions provides the needed emphasis for transformation.

EDUCATIONAL REENGINEERING

Roy Nicholson, Chairman and CEO of USA Group predicts "21st century students—and the companies and institutions that employ them—will need 21st century colleges and universities."[4]

The bottom line is that this reengineering will enable educators to serve students better.

This book examines TQI as a system with multiple processes to reengineer education. While many of the examples are from two-and four-year educational institutions, there are successful applications at all levels of education. If the faculty and staff are willing to devote the time and effort to explore how TQI fits in their environment and if the administration is willing to provide the needed commitment and resources, it will work.

A major premise of this book is that each institution should formulate its own TQI plan which reflects its culture, traditions, people, and communities. These things influence the way things happen in the institution and it doesn't make sense to ignore them by using an outside strategy or model.

The challenges facing education in the 21st century are enormous. With limited finances, offering high quality education to a changing, diverse group of learners is a major task. But the task must be accomplished or this country will again fall behind its economic competitors from the orient and northern Europe.

Since reengineering is the process of fundamentally changing the way work is performed to achieve improvements in speed, cost, and quality of service, this book calls for a systematic review of the current organization and administration of education and questions some of education's most sacred traditions. The external pressures to change education require new, bolder measures which will shake its very culture. Reengineering focuses on work and business processes and TQI is a way to affect monumental changes by involving those internal to the processes, including faculty, staff, and students.

The first several chapters of this book detail the primary components of reengineering using several examples from educational settings. This is followed by a series of success stories from institutions of various sizes and types. The excitement and enthusiasm of these educators is apparent as they report on their progress and detail their challenges.

THE NEVER-ENDING JOURNEY

To reengineer the way schools do business is to embark on a never-ending journey into the unknown. There aren't many alternatives other than responding to the challenges and viewing them as opportunities. Nicholson, in a speech to educators in New York, advised "Focusing on the needs of the customer and taking advantage of technology to improve customer service, efficiency, and productivity are two critical steps we must take in order to be competitive and in order to operate in an increasingly tough financial environment." Further, "The future is not fixed. What we do here does indeed affect the future. The best way to determine that future is to create it." [5]

By reading this book, you will gain new insights on how to create a meaningful and positive future for your educational institution.

*Total quality improvement is meeting
and exceeding customer requirements.*

Chapter 1
Introduction to
TQI in Education

This is a book about Total Quality Improvement (TQI) in education. It will help educators decide whether or not this application, first tried in business and industry, will work in their organization.

My experience gained as administrator of a two-year college during the implementation of TQI concepts, tools, and techniques in instructional programs, administration, and service departments is the basis as I relay the trials, tribulations, and challenges. While president at Fox Valley Technical College in northeastern Wisconsin, I partnered with administrators, faculty, and staff as a paradigm shift occurred. This book offers ideas for consideration by educators as they examine how TQI might be applied in their institution. While each organization is different and the implementation of total quality will be unique to the culture and climate, the concepts employed are similar.

The Fox Valley journey was a wonderful experience. The institution was reactivated and the culture was transformed as faculty and staff used TQI to refocus on fulfilling the needs of customers and continually improve the quality of their programs and services.

As USA Group National Quality Academy was formed and we began to assist others who were involved with total quality, it became obvious that much progress was being made by educators throughout the world. We will be making reference to some of these educational institutions and describing their experiences in total quality implementation. As we studied the progress in other organizations, we soon realized that some have now surpassed Fox Valley in many aspects of TQI. Chapter 7 is devoted entirely to a review of some of those success stories.

BACKGROUND

In this age of information where the use of knowledge has become a predominate factor in the world economy, education in America needs help. The world has changed and the systems used during the agriculture and industrial ages are no longer enough. U.S. students continue to lag behind their peers in other industrial countries in important subjects such as math and science. The paradox is that while recent high school graduates are better educated than previous classes, they are less prepared to enter the work force. This is not because educators have failed, but because the skills, competencies, and behaviors required by our advanced technological, information-based society have outpaced our ability to provide training within our existing structures and systems. Despite waves of reform, philosophical differences over how to achieve and measure a quality education make the target elusive. Some individuals finally give up and concede that it is impossible to improve our schools.

Despite these difficulties, there are individuals forging ahead with new programs for educational reform. Governors from several states are promoting programs of change and the Federal Department of Education is pushing for national standards and teacher competency programs to ensure that schools are improving. Some popular reform programs include those labeled school choice, site-based management, and outcome-based education. Virtually every school district is looking at alternatives to cope with the numerous challenges they face.

An Abundance of Critics

One major problem in dealing with these challenges is the realization that because practically everyone has experienced education at some time during their life, there are varied opinions about what is needed to improve education. Critics are everywhere and cries for reform are rampant, both at the local and national levels. As a result of financial and economic pressures, parents, taxpayers, and lawmakers are demanding more from the nation's schools. There is growing pressure for schools to demonstrate results as the calls for accountability multiply. There are new demands for increased teaching productivity and for documented learning outcomes. Teachers and administrators are pointing fingers at each other, criticizing their colleagues for the problems that exist. Politicians blame teachers and the unions that represent them, and parents criticize the system itself and point to educational red tape and administrators as the problems. Clearly, everyone can share part of the blame and everyone needs to be a part of making it better.

The group pushing hardest for school reform is the business community. Employers recognize that they need highly qualified workers if they are to remain competitive. Employers are requiring their workers to do more than ever before. Decision making is filtering down to the individual workstations as workers schedule their own time, measure quality, solve problems, and work in teams.

Dr. Willard R. Daggett in his *Report Card on American Education—and How to Raise the Grade,*[6] recommends that education focus on a wide array of skills, knowledge, and behaviors to form a whole range of competencies for graduates. He states that schools must put together a systematic process to move the district from where it is now to where it would like to be in the next decade. An increasing number of reformers are agreeing with Daggett.

The one common denominator that stands out during meaningful attempts for reform is the realization that major overhaul is needed in education. Piecemeal approaches have failed again and again and most reformers now agree that what is needed are monumental changes that challenge some of the long-held traditions of education. Reformers are saying that incremental improvements and minor changes are not enough. Schools can no longer take tax dollars for granted in our public institutions. They must achieve greater cost effectiveness and increased operating efficiencies if they are to survive. They must find solutions to some of the problems and challenges they face.

Cultural Transformation

Since many of the time-honored traditions of education originate in our schools of higher education, a cultural transformation must begin in our colleges and universities. Higher education has been where the deep traditions of academia originate. Our premier research universities and teacher training institutions are the centers for educational excellence. American higher education is second to none in the world and these schools of higher learning justifiably take pride in their mission of teaching and learning. However, the challenges for these institutions are complex with no easy solutions.

The problem with this *call for change* is that higher education is just starting its journey in quality. Professors, instructors, and administrators have, in the past, looked at excellence in education as based on things such as degrees, professional experience, research activities, and writing and publishing expertise. They may even look at some of the principles and practices of TQI as alien to education. Because of this inherent hesitancy, many reformers believe that faculty will not be quick to relinquish treasured traditions in academia including lifetime contracts and tenure. They believe that years will pass before TQI is universally accepted by teachers, especially in higher education.

However, many progressive education leaders are responding to the call for action. They have begun to apply some of the business prescriptions detailed in the quality movement and they have had success. Further, advanced technology is transforming the way schools operate and students learn. These technological applications, together with people-generated solutions and strategies for improvement, are occurring throughout the Country.

In a study conducted by Georgia Southern University involving four-year regionally accredited colleges and universities, 542 institutions reported that they are increasingly applying total quality management concepts on their campuses.

Of the respondents, 52% said "This institution is currently using a total quality management approach." Sixty-three percent reported that their institution is developing a plan to apply total quality management to processes.

In their report researchers state, "it can be concluded that total quality management principles can be utilized in colleges and universities to improve the quality of education and other services, as well as administrative processes." [7]

Financial pressures and external criticism encourage educators to be more receptive to change. Instructors are beginning to realize that unless they adjust their attitudes, values, and beliefs, external visions for the future will cause pressure for more than the usual cosmetic changes to existing programs and practices. They recognize that fundamental structural modifications in staffing patterns, use of technology, curriculum design, and assessment are required. While faculty will no doubt continue to be concerned about administrative motives, many now realize that TQI has the potential to be accepted in academia as a reasonable alternative to what now exists.

Essential Feedback

In the total quality effort, the needs of students and other stakeholders must be gauged and researched. Feedback from students regarding their experiences in education and the workplace is necessary. Concerns from other stakeholders and complaints must be addressed as opportunities for *moments of truth* rather than hindrances in the educational process. Educators must focus on continuous improvement and must examine whether they are using resources effectively to ensure that students have access to the latest technologies and methodologies available. Their need for support services and extracurricular activities must be reviewed.

School administrators must examine their roles and the ways that they use resources to bring about the changes necessary for continuous improvement of the educational processes. This requires more funds for faculty and staff professional development and better equipment to support and continually improve the learning processes. Since there will continue to be shortfalls in funding for education, these new requirements must be met through alternative finances and cost efficiencies. It will be easier to convince taxpayers that more resources are needed when they see institutions willing to change.

All those involved in educational decision making must realize that the teaching/learning process is central and should be geared toward future student needs. This requires a careful analysis of requirements of students and other stakeholders, including future employers.

This analysis of needs should be done carefully because narrow applications of customer service may be inappropriate. For example, it would be improper to use suggestions from students as the sole basis for determining the actual content of curriculum. In most cases, student backgrounds and experiences are limited. The best approach to improve learning systems and curriculum is to review the processes regularly and obtain feedback from students and other stakeholders external to the institution. This type of research, together with the assessment of educational outcomes, helps teachers analyze technology and determine how technological advances will be used in instruction. Teachers must examine new ways to help students achieve their objectives and must understand that continuous classroom research is essential to improving education.

Many of the examples in this book are from two-and four-year colleges and universities. However, the applications of the concepts fit at all levels of the educational continuum. The philosophy behind continuous quality improvement is based on the belief that no matter how good you are, you can still be better. This book is about vision and risk taking—trying new things that challenge our past while looking to the future.

The classrooms, laboratories, and offices of higher education are proper places to apply this philosophy and this examination. The premier programs and innovations in our colleges and universities have created an environment which attracts thousands of foreign students seeking advanced education to America. Reforms in education must analyze these successes and build on them to create the future.

Some things will have to be changed or eliminated. That's what TQI is all about—establishing systems of continuous improvement with a constant review of processes which permeate our programs and services.

DEFINITIONS

There are many definitions for reengineering and total quality improvement. Most are appropriate since the concepts are universal. Consider this definition of reengineering from Nicholson: *"Reengineering is the process of fundamentally changing the way work is performed to achieve radical improvements in speed, cost, and quality of service."*[8]

Examine this lengthy definition of total quality improvement from USA Group National Quality Academy: *"Total Quality Improvement is a management philosophy which puts systems and processes in place to meet and exceed the expectations of educational stakeholders. It is a relentless quest for continuous improvement through the use of tools and documentation in a problem-solving atmosphere that features team action and good leadership practices throughout the institution."*[9]

A simpler definition comes from Fox Valley Technical College: *"Total quality improvement is meeting and exceeding customer expectations."*[10]

With any of these definitions, the goal is to improve systems and processes by creating an atmosphere where administrators, faculty, and staff examine stakeholders' needs and carry out their functions in the most efficient manner possible.

Training and education of administrators, faculty, and staff will help ensure that the concepts, techniques, and tools behind these definitions are learned and applied. Professional development is vital to ensure that all employees remain apprised of new practices and updated teaching methodologies. Administrators and staff need to be educated in how to be more efficient in their service roles. All staff need training in TQI concepts, tools, and techniques to learn their roles and responsibilities in this quest for continuous improvement. The institution becomes, as Peter Senge suggests, a learning organization.[11] This involves a professional development focus and support for individual progress.

This support includes a firm commitment to provide resources for a total quality improvement initiative. This commitment is essential because TQI is long range, rather than short term. Employees need assurance that total quality is not just another administrative program which will whither and die. The quality theories and concepts will fit in education when all realize that application can be customized to the institution itself and that everyone has responsibility for its implementation and success.

SUMMARY COMMENTS

1. Debates about the merits of TQI in education occur among people because of a lack of understanding of what is involved.

2. Institutions which limit TQI to administrative and service applications do a disservice to the initiative.

3. Quality requires a transformation in the culture by changing the way things are done. This requires a systematic review of systems and processes, including the academic side of the institution.

4. It is essential that instructors embrace TQI and use its tools and techniques in the teaching/learning process.

5. Massive changes are required to reengineer education and create an environment which focuses on continuous improvement. The demand for quality service delivered at reduced provider cost, is becoming apparent in this era of limited finances for education.

6. The claims of both proponents and critics of TQI usually are inflated and that creates problems.

7. Some look at TQI as new words for old ideas. Others feel that continuous improvement efforts will open the doors to potential changes in such traditional areas as instructional methodology and student assessment.

8. Several issues need to be addressed as the TQI initiative begins to take hold in education. We must analyze how each of these TQI features will apply in education:

   - Serving customers
   - Reducing variations in processes
   - Decentralizing management
   - Empowering teams
   - Striving for continuous improvement
   - Institutional effectiveness
   - Conformance to requirements
   - Prevention rather than inspection
   - Management vs. Leadership
   - Zero defects management

9. Threats to change time-honored practices in academia may create an initial negative reaction. While the concepts seem to fit the times and are attractive to a growing numbers of educators, care must be taken when tampering with tradition. Therefore, the best implementation model is one in which the language and strategies are designed internally.

Chapter 2
Key Concepts of
Quality in Education

The approach presented in this book will be referred to as total quality improvement (TQI) or educational reengineering. Known by many different terms such as continuous process improvement (CPI), total quality leadership (TQL), and continuous quality improvement (CQI), its origin goes back to Walter Shewhart at Bell Laboratories in the 1930s and the use of statistical process methods in manufacturing firms beginning in the 1940s.

After World War II, TQI arrived in Japan through the teachings of Americans W. Edwards Deming, Armand Fiegenbaum, and Joseph Juran. The Japanese advocated humanistic approaches based on their belief that quality can be achieved best when there is an educated, motivated, and empowered work force. The reasons become obvious upon the examination of work and how it is organized.

Work is a process, and when viewed that way, improvement occurs best with input from everyone involved in each segment of work. With such a people-centered approach, those who perform the processes attempt to meet and exceed standards set with input from those who use or benefit from the product or service.

This customer service focus, coupled with feedback and measurement, distinguishes TQI from other forms of improvement. This aspect of TQI is often misunderstood by educators. True, customer expectations and requirements need to be met and that approach may seem alien to education since the focus in the past has often been on telling others what to do. This tradition of telling people what to do has conditioned educators to believe that they know what is best for others. The TQI ethic, on the other hand, focuses on service to others and the cornerstone is listening to what customers want.

One of the first steps in reengineering education is reviewing the key concepts of total quality improvement and examining ways to appropriately apply them in education. Quality pioneers generally agree that the elements highlighted in Table 1 are the basic components which, when linked together, form an integrated system of continuous quality improvement. As shown in Table 1, customer service emphasis is clearly at the center of it all.

Table 1—Basic Elements of Total Quality Improvement (TQI)

CUSTOMER FOCUS—THE FIRST PRIORITY

Education is a service that has customers like any other business. Those customers continually express satisfaction and dissatisfaction about the services and instruction they receive. As TQI is applied to education, customers are identified and feedback mechanisms are established to help determine their specific needs. Customer data is then analyzed to determine how well customer expectations have been met. In this way, educators learn what constitutes quality in the eyes of its past, current, and future customers. The goal of TQI is to deliver what is necessary to meet and exceed those expectations.

Who is education intended to benefit? There have been many debates about that. Students are usually looked at as being education's primary customers, however, the supplier/customer relationship is somewhat different from that of a hotel or restaurant.

In education, TQI is applied as the teacher determines the needs of students and then balances those needs with the needs of other stakeholders (customers). These stakeholders include employers who hire graduates as well as other educators who will provide advanced instruction in the future. In this process, the instructor uses experience and expertise in analyzing the expectations of the various stakeholders and determining how best to use that information in a customer service way. The instructor is viewed as a customer in internal processes when he/she receives services from others. The administration and service department staff become suppliers who provide services to both students and instructors. The ultimate goal is to improve processes and systems by obtaining feedback from the different stakeholders and then exceeding their expectations.

The stakeholders or customers in education are of two types: external (students, employers, parents, taxpayers, other educators from different institutions, board members, the community at large) and internal (other instructors, administrators, service department staff).

This service focus does not necessarily mean that students and others are given whatever they want. For example, even though administrators are suppliers of services to faculty and staff and may wish to meet all their requests, not all needs can be provided. In this context, administrators view requests from customers throughout the organization and establish priorities while considering external influences and possible constraints. Likewise, the teacher examines feedback from students and then balances their expectations and needs with those from other stakeholders. In both cases, the supplier uses certain leadership skills to balance needs from various stakeholders.

Another customer service technique often used in TQI is *competitive benchmarking*. This process involves studying the best practices of other organizations by systematically observing the external practices and implementing those found to be most applicable. For example, the TQI process itself can be improved using competitive benchmarking to study world-class TQI organizations and then implement those aspects found to be best suited to the culture of the organization. The TQI process itself offers great opportunities for benchmarking as a means for sharing successes and challenges. While each institution should design a TQI model unique to itself, there are many ideas and strategies which can be obtained from others and replicated using the benchmarking process.

Contrary to the beliefs of some educators, administrators and teachers do not relinquish their professional responsibilities because of these types of customer service application. The process involves reviewing requests and input from various stakeholder groups in light of existing circumstances. Then, decisions are made based on the data collected. For example, the instructor still assumes overall responsibility for determining appropriate course content and teaching methods. While the student and others have input, the instructor remains responsible for defining learning standards and providing appropriate learning activities to ensure that the standards are met. In this system, learning objectives are established and met through the application of tested quality tools and effective teaching strategies determined and evaluated using customer service techniques.

An important component of this customer service focus is the requirement that the mission and common directions of the institution are articulated to give purpose and a sense of accomplishment to the process. A clear, succinctly written mission statement is an essential part of TQI. The goal is to have everyone in the institution understand the mission and become focused on meeting it.

Each instructional program and every service department should also have a written mission statement to complement the central mission of the organization. This helps everyone to know what to aim for. A clearly stated mission may also be written for each class and become a part of a complex network of goals communicated to all.

LEADERSHIP—THE ULTIMATE COMMITMENT

Another key element of TQI is leadership. Senior administrators must provide the visionary leadership and commitment needed in the TQI effort. This top-level buy-in and support is essential to show everyone that the top school leaders support the quality improvement initiative. In the beginning, top administrators identify priorities and design action plans and then seek endorsement by the faculty and staff. They gain assistance and support from middle managers and faculty leaders who are in critical positions, usually being the closest to those who directly serve students.

Table 2—Basic Element—Leadership

This visionary leadership differs from traditional management and that changes the usual practices and transforms the culture of the institution. Administrators, managers, and faculty leaders take on new roles which center on shared decision making with maximum input from others. In this environment, there is friendly collaboration and empowerment in a less hierarchical and more integrated system.

These progressive leadership styles, now appearing throughout the institution, are marked departures from traditional bureaucracies with top-to-bottom control. Traditional management approaches foster accountability and authority, however, it usually results in lost effectiveness, efficiency, and spirit because of the control imposed by those in charge.

The reengineered TQI culture encourages educators, staff, and students to own their work and take responsibility for learning with a shared mission and purpose. A nonthreatening environment focuses on the sharing of power, ownership, and authority, built on new trust levels. Leadership styles such as these are encouraged throughout the organization to gain mutual understanding of the aims of the unit (institution, department, classroom, service area), recognizing the assistance provided by others to enhance this new culture. Leadership styles such as these become the preferred model for the classroom, as instructors and staff learn and apply the same types of new management skills.

In this mutually supportive environment, teachers and administrators become servant leaders as they provide instruction and service to others. All soon realize that their individual successes are interlocked with team action; their achievements rise and fall together. In every department, classroom, and work unit of the school, envisioning, integrating, and enabling replaces controlling, directing, and executing. A reengineered environment is the result.

TEAM PROBLEM SOLVING—CORNERSTONE OF TQI

The new quality culture requires renewed and genuine teamwork. Lasting and significant changes simply will not work unless instructors and other staff are directly and actively involved in the planning and development of desired changes. Such involvement by people closest to the customer (teacher to student, service worker to clients, administrators and supervisors to associates) is paramount to the success of TQI.

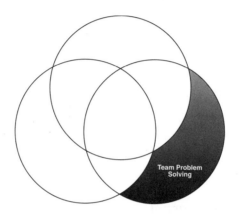

Table 3—Basic Element—Team Problem Solving

These teams work together toward common ends and become the cornerstone of TQI as they review processes, determine problems, find their root causes, and try to solve them permanently. Team members have the expertise because they are usually closest to the customer. They solve problems by documenting the processes of the work they are studying and using teamwork skills to build consensus around issues while eliminating the causes of the problems in a systematic way. In its simplest form, this teamwork can best be defined as joint action by a group in which each individual subordinates his or her interests and opinions to the unity and interests of the group. Effective teamwork is required if problems are to be solved and meaningful changes are to occur in education.

The goal is to develop teams which are more effective and stronger than the sum of their individual members. This requires a breakdown of subcultures usually present in our educational institutions. These subcultures in departments and work units often develop policies and procedures that safeguard their own interests. Competition emerges as members are ranked and rewarded based on comparison with others.

TQI seeks to eliminate these practices and foster improvement by reviewing and streamlining processes that cross department lines. Cooperation is sought as teachers, executives, department chairs, and other stakeholders become involved in identifying, analyzing, and correcting problems.

These same problem-solving techniques and tools are learned by students as they engage in problem solving in student teams, under the leadership of the instructors. One goal in the application of TQI is to eliminate inappropriate competition among students by doing away with comparisons and creating respect and trust. These TQI principles and techniques, taught to students, become micro applications of quality modeled by teachers and practiced by students.

These upgraded and integrated systems seek to improve the whole institution without ignoring individual or department accomplishments. An environment of continuous improvement is sought with proactive and dynamic approaches that foster improved interrelationships. The entire organization is viewed as a system with hundreds of processes, all subject to review, analysis, and change. This continuous improvement philosophy, applied to teaching and learning, requires the constant review of all instructional processes. Curriculum and instruction and the other supportive processes, usually referred to as student services, are under constant review by the faculty and staff.

METHODS AND TOOLS—PROCESS MANAGEMENT AT WORK

TQI methodology and tools are primary features of another basic quality element sometimes referred to as process management. In the quality-based institution, scientific approaches and the use of the correct tools enhance decision making as the teams plan, implement, and monitor the solutions being tried. In this problem-solving environment, the use of data is important to ensure that appropriate systems are designed and faulty ones are corrected while avoiding temporary fixes. These new methods examine root causes of problems with the goal of eliminating them forever. Statistical tools are used to assist in the analysis and monitor the proposed solutions.

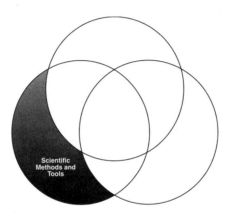

Table 4—Basic Element—Process Management

The tools and techniques commonly used in problem solving were referred to by Deming as the *seven basic tools*. They include flowcharts, cause and effect diagrams, histograms, Pareto charts, run charts, scatter diagrams, and control charts. There are also data collection tools such as surveys, focus group research, and individual interviews with customers. Several planning tools are used to determine strategic directions, set goals, and prepare action plans.

The Plan-Do-Check-Act (PDCA) cycle is followed and a system of on-going monitoring and assessment is needed.

Even though the primary focus of quality is on prevention rather than inspection, standards are needed as benchmarks for the entire organization. These effectiveness standards are used as targets for improvement and frequently are adjusted upward in a dynamic environment of continuous quality improvement.

MEANINGFUL DATA—NO MORE
MANAGEMENT BY GENIUS

Another component of TQI is the use of meaningful data to solve problems and make decisions. Data must be carefully collected and analyzed using effective information systems. No longer can educators depend on antiquated computer systems used to collect and compile student and staff information. Often, these systems were designed to meet state or federal requirements and controls for reporting. This resulted in a series of computer generated reports prepared to meet external guidelines. These reports often became barriers which led to ineffective internal information and communication. These traditional information systems must change, and the TQI process will help make the changes more efficient and effective.

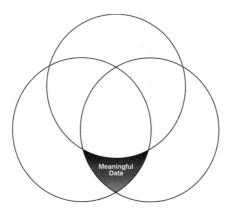

Table 5—Basic Element—Information System

In the preferred data collection and analysis environment, data is gathered to determine and document user (customer) needs and is then disseminated to individuals and teams following a set distribution plan. For example, information is disseminated to faculty and staff in carefully prepared reports using concise data useful for improving learning systems.

This transformed information system calculates the extent of improvement in the institution. The use of valid data and the sharing of information is basic to a TQI culture. Therefore, a major shift occurs in data collection, compilation, and dissemination as everyone gains access to information which, in the past, had been reserved for only a select group of senior administrators. This sharing becomes important as it assists individuals and teams in their planning, documenting, and problem-solving efforts.

ORGANIZATIONAL CLIMATE—
A CULTURAL TRANSFORMATION

A transformed institutional culture and climate is one of the expected outcomes in the quality-based institution. People soon become seen as the most important resource. Administrators, faculty, and staff are given the training, tools, and authority to create changes need for meaningful reform in the institution. TQI becomes the vehicle for systematic and continual improvement and changes are based on the needs of internal and external customers. New leadership skills emerge as managers and administrators learn to facilitate, empower, coach, and enable others. A virtual revolution occurs as institutional networking and accountability replace department focus and individuality. A learning organization emerges as the need for continuous upgrading and education becomes apparent.

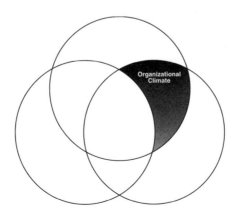

Table 6—Basic Element—Organizational Climate

In such a mutually supportive environment, faculty and staff become more involved in shaping and monitoring the mission, purpose, and strategic directions of the institution. This involvement results in positive changes in morale as a negative, complaining, and finger-pointing atmosphere is replaced with trust and mutual respect based on integrity and professionalism. This new organizational climate results in improved conditions for both students and staff.

An emphasis and focus on the human development aspects of quality has often been ignored in halfhearted efforts directed largely on statistically-controlled accountability systems. Measurement and accountability are highlighted and the individual is largely ignored. The preferred approach is balanced and involves accountability and human development components working together to create positive change. This balance sets the stage for further improvement through team building, consensus reaching, and conflict resolution. Operational guidelines and standards are agreed upon to define responsibilities, enhance cooperation, and foster partnerships.

This cultural transformation occurs over time and requires commitment, understanding, and patience. It won't happen overnight. Administrators need to loosen the management reins and give up control. That may be difficult because administrators and managers may have been rewarded in the past for controlling people. Similarly, instructors may have been conditioned to use practices inconsistent with TQI. Changes at first will be gradual and uneven in application and they won't become permanent and meaningful until people at all levels find that team efforts with ongoing communications work best. Managers learn the delicate balance between the application of TQI techniques, tools, and strategies, and the human/social aspects which focus on respect, dignity, and worth of all individuals. Leaders who find this balance between the two approaches will experience a successful cultural transformation that features a gradual improvement in relationships.

EDUCATION AND TRAINING—
THE LEARNING ORGANIZATION

One element that distinguishes TQI organizations is the focus on the individual upgrading and development of employees. Those in charge soon realize that they can gain the competitive advantage by having people who are well trained and up to date. These leaders know that a well trained team of individuals will lead to a reengineering whereby the institution evolves as a learning organization with education and training as an on-going activity. Every individual from the chief administrator to every personnel level needs an individualized plan for development. Table 7 shows an ideal approach with a plan that includes four developmental areas: academic/technical upgrading, TQI application training, specialized training, and enrichment and family development training.

Table 7—Individualized Professional Development Model

In this model, each person is expected to be academically and technically competent in his/her specialty (teaching, managing, service, technical). Without this upgrading, staff can become complacent, the curriculum will become outdated, and the technical and management staff will fall behind.

In the second section of the model, TQI application training keeps the process going and links staff together with a constant purpose. This training focuses on the institutional commitment to TQI and keeps individuals current in the topics related to the movement. Everyone participates in this training because of its importance at each personnel level (teaching, administrative, service). Specialized training, shown in the third section of the model, is also offered based on the individual requirements and responsibilities of people in the organization.

The enrichment and family development training focuses on individual, physical, emotional, and family relationships, using TQI techniques and tools. The physical and mental health of employees and their families is vital to the well being of the institution for it leads to greater productivity by the staff members.

Therefore, the ideal staff development program is comprehensive and individualized with TQI instruction integrated with career enhancement. This learning organization philosophy is accepted and universally used by quality driven organizations.

Through this training, faculty and staff begin to understand the basic components of the quality improvement process. It is necessary because of misunderstandings about quality improvement systems. Some faculty and staff have a problem with the TQI language. For example, they have difficulty referring to students as customers. They feel the business language of TQI is inappropriate for educational institutions. Even the name Total Quality Management is offensive and other terms such as benchmarking, statistical process control, Hoshin planning, and customer service make educators uncomfortable.

Another difficulty encountered in the beginning is the model for implementation and the strategies used to foster involvement. Opponents may disagree with the various stages of the plan as the process is initiated. Training programs may be criticized by some who feel the approach is not consistent with the philosophy of one or the other pioneers of quality. Debate may center around the sequence of events and the emphasis given to the components of TQI.

The final problem is related to commitment by the administration. Faculty and staff are tired of programs and reforms which have been tried and abandoned. They are suspect of anything which requires change in the way things have always been done and they wonder if the administration will continue to support the change over time.

Training programs, properly planned and conducted, can address the problems mentioned early in the process of implementation. Through the training programs, facilitators can meet the challenges before they surface. The inevitable controversy which occurs when implementing change of this magnitude can be limited by recognizing that some discussion and debate is healthy and needed. Forums for debate should be provided and discussion about the issues should be encouraged.

Because of these inevitable challenges, some leaders choose to implement TQI on a partial or piecemeal basis. Limited applications tend to focus on a few aspects of the overall TQI model. These are generally piecemeal programs which become popular because they are easier to start. Some examples include outcome-based education, site-based management, quality circles, statistical process control, team-centered management, teacher empowerment, accelerated learning, customer service, and principle-centered leadership. Usually, one or two of these are tried and most often, these isolated approaches are not successful. They follow the usual dismal path of educational fads that soon go away.

Table 8 shows some of these short-term applications. Note that they fit logically under the umbrella of the comprehensive TQI model. Very often, these limited efforts achieve early success. However, before long, the limited nature of the idea causes it to weaken and disappear.

Table 8—TQI Umbrella of Short-Term Programs

The relationship of TQI to the assessment process is another issue that comes up and should be addressed during training. Assessment is an important component of TQI which requires that measurement criteria are clearly stated. Measurement *indicators* are used as benchmarks when analyzing progress. The controversial aspect of assessment relates to the mechanism or format used as the standards. Three commonly used standards are the Malcolm Baldrige Examination Standards, the Presidential Quality Award Criteria, and the International Organization for Standardization Registration (ISO 9000 Series).

The Malcolm Baldrige Examination Standards were developed by the US Government to recognize companies in the United States which excel in quality achievement and quality management. The Award promotes awareness of TQI, an understanding of its requirements, and a sharing of successful strategies derived during implementation. The standards are used to help summarize the strengths, determine areas for improvement, and identify successful management styles. The standards may be used as objective means of evaluating an organization's total quality system. The Presidential Quality Award Criteria, designed for use in governmental agencies, are similar to Malcolm Baldrige Examination. Both of these evaluation systems have been used by educational institutions to assess their application of TQI.

ISO 9000 is a series of quality system standards developed by the International Organization for Standardization in Switzerland. The standards give consumers a common base for comparison. Many customers from Europe, Canada, and the United States require ISO 9000 registration from the manufacturers of products they purchase.

The standardization formats have many similarities. They all use criteria established for comparison and assessment purposes with definable standards used as benchmarks for self assessment and analysis. They are used by different types of organizations to announce to customers that they are committed to Total Quality Improvement. None have been successfully adapted and accepted in education, except on an institution by institution basis.

This interest in national and state standards and the continual demand for comparative criteria may result in a set of measurable indicators of excellence in education. Many educators believe that national and state standards are not the answer. They believe that the best criteria are standards unique to each institution and designed by internal staff with help from external stakeholders. In a survey conducted by Georgia Southern University in 1993 and completed by 542 four-year colleges and universities, 84% felt that unique quality award criteria should be developed. Only 11% reported that they believe quality cannot be measured.[12] A set of national policies which promote reform in education through TQI and demand major change in the way things are done may work. However, unique criteria created by the faculty, staff, and customers of each institution will probably best serve the institution in its quest for excellence.

CONTINUOUS IMPROVEMENT—
THE ULTIMATE GOAL

The umbrella over all these quality elements and components is the concept of continuous improvement. It recognizes that quality levels reached today won't be good enough tomorrow. It requires that indicators of excellence and institutional effectiveness be constantly upgraded. Continuous improvement demands that the institution systematically examine and constantly monitor processes valued by customers. It puts a stop to business as usual as the focus shifts to paying attention to the needs and expectations of others. This concept is so critical to quality initiatives that some experts call the entire TQI process by names such as *continuous process improvement* or *quality process improvement*. Colleges where continuous quality improvement flourishes report high motivation among the faculty and staff to do the best work possible in an atmosphere of dynamic change.

SUMMARY COMMENTS

1. Design a model unique to your institution, its mission, purpose, strategic directions, and values.

2. Recognize that there is no one right way to implement total quality improvement.

3. Adhere to Deming's teaching—"All models are wrong, but some may be useful."

4. The central focus of any quality model is customer service. It is essential to design feedback vehicles to determine customer expectations and needs.

5. The basic principles and concepts of total quality are universally accepted without much debate. It is the language of quality and the strategies used to implement which create debate and disagreement.

Chapter 3
Leadership and
the Use of Teams

Administrators commitment to the quality improvement process must be obvious to the entire staff. Visible actions send an unmistakable message about what is important and where priorities lie. TQI causes a major shift in the way things are done in administration, service, and instructional program areas and also in the way teams use decision making.

Good leadership in work units and instructional departments results in effective teamwork, cooperation, and communication. Involving people in decisions, encouraging participation in problem solving, sharing information, and providing constructive feedback becomes a way of life. The quality process recognizes and builds on the contributions of all: teachers, administrators, service managers, and service staff.

Hopefully, the first visible signs of major change during this cultural transformation occur at the administrative areas of the institution. Senior executives change from being enforcers or directors to being facilitators who educate, advise, empower, enable, and support people. This new administrative culture creates patterns with the central focus shifting to the priorities of the customers.

Robert Carothers refers to this shift from traditional management as *servant leadership*. Leaders are viewed as being servants first and in that role they articulate goals, inspire trust, listen, and provide positive feedback. The ability to maximize the talents and potential of all groups of people becomes paramount. School administrators become servant leaders to the faculty and staff and instructors become servant leaders to students.[13]

The *servant leader* concept promotes respect in a culture that is diversified, more inclusive, and equitable. Differences are valued and encouraged, and multicultural strengths are displayed. This *leading through serving* philosophy requires new skills that focus on listening, consensus reaching, decision making, and conflict resolution. The result is an institution with a spirit of togetherness and sharing that exists for all the people. The goal of the leader is to allow people to be autonomous and free. This atmosphere of caring and quality of relationships leads to the sharing of power and involvement of many in decision making. A network of learning from each other evolves.

How can these leadership styles be fostered in education? What steps can administrators take to create this new environment? It won't be easy and it won't happen overnight, but over time the typical hierarchical organizational structures of the institution will weaken and shift toward more shared decision making.

Some reform movements change the way things are done while maintaining traditional organizational structures. TQI is different in that it requires gradual changes in organizational structures to foster the decision-making capabilities of all people in the institution—instructors, middle managers, service and classified staff, and administrators. There is no quick and easy way to do this as it usually takes time for those in charge to recognize that shared decision making will probably reduce the layers in the hierarchy. Fewer *line* positions and more *staff* or resource people are needed. Usually, this results in fewer senior executives and more *staff* positions at lower levels.

Ideally, as TQI matures and senior administrators become more comfortable with the changes in culture, autonomous departments are created and staff have greater authority. Some schools adopt a concept called *site-based* management.

This is more prevalent at the elementary and secondary levels as principals are given greater authority over processes formerly handled by senior administrators of the school district. This shift in authority results in team-centered approaches used in facility management, personnel recruitment, selection, orientation, curriculum redesign, and other management functions formerly centered in top administration. The same system can be applied in higher education as instructional divisions and service departments receive greater autonomy in administrative functions reached using an agreed-upon decision-making model. The college administration delegates greater authority to departments. In this model, top executives loosen the reins and relinquish much of their authority as they become resources to departments they may have previously controlled.

This type of administrative leadership evolves over time because some people believe that with this customer-service model, executives, supervisors, and managers will be compelled to turn over many of their responsibilities to frontline service workers. When properly applied, this will not happen because administrative, service, and faculty leaders have many responsibilities that cannot be delegated. The college president, for example, has responsibilities related to institutional accountability that cannot be turned over to others, even though input and feedback may be solicited from faculty and staff. Likewise, the teacher has many responsibilities related to content determination, classroom management, and teaching, that cannot and should not be turned over to students. The goal is to encourage executives, service managers, deans, principals, and faculty, to develop a customer service approach that examines the needs and expectations of customers while maintaining primary responsibilities. The main cultural change is that there is continued input from all customers and stakeholders as a part of the decision-making process.

All this leads to greater involvement by people closest to the customer (faculty to students, service workers to customers) and this is paramount to the success of quality improvement. The primary strategy used to achieve this is the establishment of a network of teams.

Teams are groups of people who work together toward common ends. They become the cornerstone of the quality process. There are two types of teams found in education—self-managed teams and cross-functional teams. Self-managed teams evolve in departments and work units of the institution as faculty and staff go through a series of stages. At each stage of the process, teams assume greater authority and responsibility as they systematically prepare for self-management. The movement toward becoming a self-managed team requires the team to work through a series of processes at each stage.

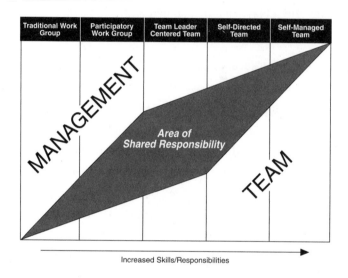

Table 9—Stages of Development—Self-Managed Teams

Departmental and instructional processes are defined and flowcharted and problems are identified and solved by teams.

Cross-functional teams are organized to attack institution-wide problems. The progress made in solving problems and settling key issues depends to a large extent on the ability to create and foster effective teams of teachers, managers, and service staff.

This may require changes in the structure and nature of institutional governance. As TQI reaches maturity in the organization, policies and governance structures are reviewed to determine if they are effective. Team involvement creates changes in the way decisions are reached. In the past, administrators may have been rewarded for controlling people. Now, with the use of teams, they are asked to change. Meanwhile, some people may expect administrators to continue as they have managed in the past, taking charge of things and functioning in traditional ways. They prefer control-type administrators and the old ways.

Because of this and for other reasons, some administrators may want to take over control again and revert back to decision-making styles of the past. That creates problems because team members get discouraged when administrators are unwilling to delegate authority and involve teams in performing their roles and functions.

TEAMWORK DEFINED

Teamwork is the joint action by a group of people whereby each person relinquishes his or her individual interests, opinions, and actions to the efficiency of the group. This requires mutual sharing and involvement in an atmosphere of trust and unselfishness. Teamwork flourishes where there is respect for opinions and rights of others with open communication. In this participative environment, team members share experiences, abilities, opinions, and concerns.

Teams can best solve problems because they usually have the expertise and are closest to the unit of work itself. They solve problems by building consensus around issues. Since they are most often the ones affected, it is common sense to ask them to participate in the resolution of their own problems.

In its simplest form, each individual on a team subordinates his or her interests and opinions to the unity and interests of the group. This means that teamwork, participation, and involvement are integral concepts. Teams reach maturity when an atmosphere of trust and unselfishness exists among members. In such an environment, open communication and respect for opinions and rights of others are paramount.

The success of quality improvement efforts in schools depends on the ability of the administration to provide leadership and creates and fosters cohesive teams of teachers, managers, and service staff. It is important, then, to examine the desired characteristics of productive teams and set systems in place to prepare team members to be successful.

People will become motivated when they are comfortable in their work and confident that their job is important. As teams design their goals, they need to have support and be recognized for their accomplishments. They need to have a sense of control and influence and be involved in meaningful and relevant issues. These favorable conditions, fostered by school leaders, influence team performance.

Teams must be able to trust other members of the team and those in leadership positions. Unless there is trust, it is fruitless to ask teachers and staff to contribute their ideas, energy, and time. Trust occurs most easily in a supportive environment where there is understanding and the recognition that there will be differences of opinion. In this supportive environment, risk taking is encouraged and failures are recognized as opportunities for future growth.

Trust develops over time as top management recognizes the important roles of teams in creating meaningful and lasting changes. Trust also develops when administrators shift from traditional practices of *telling* to new practices of *listening*. The skill of effective *listening* becomes a primary requirement for managers in the team environment.

Team members also need to change the way they do things. Since members are expected to assume authority they haven't been accustomed to having, they must learn to accept more responsibility and be accountable for their actions. Documentation is needed and effective communication is required to ensure that all know what is happening and who is going to be responsible for doing different things. A clear set of written operational guidelines is the best way to guarantee this.

Preparation and training in team building is needed to help teams become effective. It's a good idea to have several individuals in the organization trained as team facilitators and available to assist teams as they move through the various stages of development.

As top management prepares to establish teams and delegate more authority to them, there are some important questions to answer:

- Is there administrative support for the use of teams?

- Are the team members ready for shared management responsibilities?

- Has there been training in team building, communications, and conflict resolution?

- Can an atmosphere of trust, confidence, and loyalty be attained?

- Are the teams willing to be involved in risk taking, problem solving, and self-directed management?

SUMMARY COMMENTS

1. Significant changes and innovation in education will not occur unless the faculty and staff are directly and actively involved in the planning and development of desired change and in the decision-making activities of the institution.

2. All individuals should be given opportunities to participate in the quality process through involvement on work unit, departmental, and cross functional teams.

3. The effective use of teams results in a shift in the way that top executives and board members function.

4. As cross-functional teams are organized, they need guidelines, parameters, and timelines. The teams should also know, beforehand, how their recommendations will be used by the administration.

5. The manager is still very important as he/she creates an ideal environment to foster cohesive teams of teachers, service staff, and managers. The perfect atmosphere is one where people feel comfortable, confident, and motivated to do their job as team members. At the center of it all is effective communication.

6. Because the team process requires a clarification of issues, ideas, and suggestions, conflict often occurs naturally and needs to be handled in constructive and nonthreatening ways. Every person should have opportunities to express opinions.

7. Because of the special skills needed by the team members and their managers, adequate training in team building and conflict resolution is necessary and facilitation may be required.

8. Effective leaders create many other leaders in the institution.

9. The best leaders encourage innovation, share credit, and drive out sources of fear.

10. Leaders recognize that people are their most important resource.

Chapter 4
Using Total Quality
to Improve Teaching

While there are advantages and cost savings for service departments to be customer oriented and focused on increased productivity, the real impact of TQI in education will come from the instructional departments. Unfortunately, there are only a few widely publicized examples of TQI efforts in the classroom. In fact, there is a perception that faculty are resistant to TQI and other ideas for improvement coming from the business world.

Many people believe that teachers don't want to change. This skepticism among critics about the lack of flexibility and adaptability is usually generalized as instructors are viewed as being traditionalists unwilling to try approaches advocated by TQI. Because of these perceptions, some board members and administrators don't even attempt to promote initiatives such as quality improvement.

In spite of this skepticism, there may be a perfect fit between teaching and the total quality movement. Most instructors are continually looking for ways to improve their material and methods. They have chosen teaching careers because they are interested in helping people and their motivation stems from watching students successfully advance in the learning process.

The very culture of instruction centers around fostering quality by improving the teaching process, maintaining a research orientation, updating and redesigning curriculum, and improving evaluation and assessment practices. These quality improvement functions are already priorities for most instructors.

Also, because a basic concept of TQI is to encourage people to manage themselves, faculty in their self-contained classrooms are already involved in self management. For these reasons and others, most teachers accept quality concepts once they are convinced that TQI will not diminish their responsibilities as teachers or interfere with academic freedom.

Why then has the concept of TQI implementation in education been largely ignored in instruction? If the quality of education is impacted most in classrooms and teachers are relatively free to change the way they teach, why don't teachers use total quality improvement processes to improve their teaching, revise their curricula, maintain their research orientation, and update their evaluation systems? Why is there reluctance by many instructors to support TQI?

Perhaps this hesitancy is somewhat related to academic tradition because the quality movement is usually coupled with demands to change time-honored practices. Maybe it's because the idea originated outside of academia in the business world. Or perhaps teachers are just fed up with new ideas that become fads that are short-term and disappear when there are changes in administration or federal and state initiatives.

In spite of these challenges, I believe that it is possible to use quality processes, techniques, and tools to improve teaching. After all, two of the basic tenants of TQI include encouraging shared decision making and giving people the freedom to make necessary changes in their work processes. Faculty have always wanted more latitude to make changes and this may be an attractive vehicle to give them greater freedom. They also want to be more involved in planning and decision making. They are aware that new technology, changing economic and social conditions, and pressure for greater accountability are producing more demands for change. Enrollment cutbacks, downsizing, increased class sizes, and other efforts to contain costs can create trauma and discontent with profound effects on their institutions.

Faculty are not pleased with all this discontent and are starting to realize that the elements of quality improvement are generally consistent with their theories of teaching and learning. As a result, some educational institutions are moving aggressively to foster continuous improvement using formal quality practices.

WHY SOME SCHOOLS ARE SUCCESSFUL

Reports continue to circulate about schools effectively managing change by adapting their environment using quality systems and strategies from the private sector. These institutions are somehow surviving downsizing, program cuts, declining services, and other drastic changes resulting from problems related to dwindling finances.

What causes these organizations to be successful while others decline? There are many factors but there appear to be three distinguishing variables. Successful organization have:

- Strong institutional leadership.
- Continuous review of service and instructional processes.
- Greater faculty and staff involvement in decision making.

An examination of these variables reveals that they likewise impact on the teaching/learning processes.

These institutions believe that old models of leadership, driven by strategies of control and based on power, will not work anymore. They have found that authority and power are less important today and that influence, empowerment, and persuasion seem to work best. Leadership in these progressive institutions flows from those one leads. Students, faculty, and staff are treated differently then before. In this refined customer service model, these groups are served in ways in which they define their own needs and expectations. The worth of all individuals is recognized by applying human resource traits such as caring and understanding. Leaders throughout the institution seek to make others capable and competent through empowerment that gives confidence to students, faculty, and staff while allowing them to act on their own. Students and service staff become partners with instructors and administrators who adapt new styles of leadership to try to continuously improve.

In these schools, faculty and staff continually review their systems and processes and make changes as necessary. They are always redefining what they do with the processes they are responsible for. They are never satisfied with the status quo and as they are always looking for ways to do things. They use problem solving approaches to examine issues while applying scientific methodology and solid research before making major changes. They follow the Plan-Do-Check-Act (PDCA) cycle to foster systemic growth across the institution.

Decisions are made after compiling, charting, and analyzing data, rather than relying on intuition, experience, and guesswork. Measurement tools, usually found in the private sector, are adapted and used with a focus on continuous improvement.

The third variable of successful schools is related to the others because it calls for active involvement by faculty and staffing in planning, budgeting, and decision making. Administrators, managers, faculty, and staff become partners in moving the organization forward. This partnering among personnel levels is more than passive involvement as there is active participation throughout the organization.

These institutions have found that many of the tenants and practices of total quality have been present in the past. The principles are found in most schools, though often in isolated departments or classrooms. The main change brought about by the implementation of total quality is the institution-wide application as everyone begins to look at things with a systemic rather than departmental or individual approach. These adaptations in education are causing more and more educators to look at quality as a means to improve.

In fact, there seems to be a scramble by institutions to get started with some form of quality improvement programs. According to the American Council on Education annual 1993 Campus Trends survey and a 1993 *Business Week* survey, between 60–70 percent of college presidents were engaged in some form of total quality improvement efforts, compared to less than 12 percent in 1991.[14]

The efforts to implement TQI are now increasing due to many factors. Critics point to double-digit percentage tuition increases, out-of-control costs, increasingly dissatisfied publics, and distrust as reasons why education is more receptive to change. TQI is often viewed as something completely new, however, and only a few brave institutions have implemented quality across the organization in administration, service, and instruction. Some instructional applications have been tried and a review of these may be helpful to others considering entering the world of TQI in academia. This chapter discusses some of the changes occurring in the classroom setting. Chapter 7 presents several case studies for examination.

The same components and skills of exemplary leadership, constant review of processes, and input from stakeholders can be applied as well in classrooms. Instructors with training and experiences in quality techniques and tools can use these facilitative skills as they cope with problems and challenges they face. Some teachers thrive on change using quality as the change vehicle. At the same time, other faculty, even some on the same campus, become frustrated and bitter about similar problems.

What causes some instructors to successfully cope with problems, while others despair and become frustrated? Why do some teachers constantly complain about things while others are content to deal with problems and challenges with enthusiasm and professionalism?

The answers are complex and not unlike those found when discussing successful schools and administrative leadership. These same factors are being used in efforts to improve instruction. The following application examples of TQI principles, tools, and techniques being used in the teaching/learning processes demonstrate this similarity.

CHANGING FUNCTIONS OF TEACHERS

Since teachers have the most control over what happens during instruction, their input is essential when considering direct application of TQI in the learning environment. The methods used and learning principles employed are based on teacher experiences and educational backgrounds. This has often lead to great differences in the caliber of teaching which students receive. Some instructors rely heavily on lecture as a way to disseminate information. Others use media and computer technology. Still others rely on students to control their own learning through independent study and work with teams.

This teacher control over the teaching/learning process distinguishes education from other organizations which implement TQI. In the private sector, front-line deliverers of services follow sets of standards usually designed by managers or foremen. It is different in education as teachers usually set their own standards.

TQI encourages more research to determine what works best to improve learning efficiency. The current research supports some of the following applications of TQI to improve learning efficiency. There are several examples of successful applications of TQI that have made a difference in the classroom. These are detailed here to assist teachers in selecting what works best for them.

Teachers as Leaders

Instructors often use new leadership styles and practices as they shift toward more facilitative approaches with students. They become more service oriented in a transformed classroom culture. Being persuasive rather than directive, customer driven rather than controlling, and empowering rather than directing are characteristics usually found in these teachers. The same leadership techniques and practices teachers expect from top administrators are demonstrated when the teachers work with students.

Instructors become coaches, planners, counselors, advisors, problem solvers, and partners with students in this new culture. They use integrated networks rather than top-down communication and view mistakes by students as part of their growth and development. They try to eliminate fear, mistrust, and anxiety usually present in autocratic approaches in the teaching/learning process. In this student-centered environment, instructors use teamwork, leadership skills, and other practices they would like to see modeled by others in authority. They plan activities to encourage students to use the same leadership skills as a part of the learning process. The goal is to have students become facilitators and student teachers, thereby developing positive leadership traits.

Continuous Improvement

The *constant process review* feature of quality also applies as teachers focus on continuous review of processes to detect problems and eliminate them forever. Teachers use principles, techniques, and tools of TQI to set their course of action and design their own systems for improvement. They partner with service workers and administrators to install new ways to solve problems and improve learning.

In this way, they use and model continuous process improvement techniques in the classroom setting and establish criteria for students to use the same tools and techniques during the learning process. The goal is to graduate individuals with TQI competencies by engaging students in solving problems through the use of quality tools and techniques. This provides them with a new set of quality competencies to use after graduation. Students learn that they can best solve problems working in teams. Quick-fix solutions, doomed to fail, are substituted with systematic approaches and process management applications.

Working in teams, students solve instructional problems using scientific methods and statistical approaches. They learn that teams can effectively use conflict resolution and consensus-building skills to reach decisions. In the TQI-oriented classroom, students learn to appreciate the strengths and capabilities of other team members as well as the diversity of their peers. As a result, students experience the power of the process.

Classroom Guidelines

Teachers partner with students to jointly establish guidelines for classroom management and operations, while considering the needs and expectations of each other. Teachers discover that the TQI ethic of service and respect means listening more and employing techniques of good customer service. This may be difficult at first because, by tradition, educators may have believed that they know what is best for their students. The attitude of *serving others* places a new recognition on the worth of individuals, with caring and understanding for each other gained through intensive listening. Students and faculty, in this environment, become partners in sharing their vision and experiences to form agreements and establish requirements related to classroom and personal management. This relationship is based on the belief that unless there are significant and long-lasting changes in the way that teachers and students interact, the real problems which face education will continue to grow. This change imposes greater responsibilities on students and teachers.

Functional Analysis Matrix

It is practically impossible for a teacher to be completely qualified in all of the responsibilities usually defined in their job descriptions. Teachers are expected to be curriculum planners and designers, lecturers, managers, schedulers, counselors, diagnosticians, advisers, technology experts, statisticians, and evaluators. Teachers are also expected to have skills in group work, problem solving, distance learning, conflict resolution, computer-based instruction, and accelerated learning. In short, teachers are asked to be *super people*. While many teachers are competent in several of these functions, most are limited in their abilities to perform all that is expected of them. As a result, teachers are often criticized by those who have different ideas about what is expected from teachers.

A process used to chart these functions is a matrix diagram completed by teachers. A sample *functional analysis* matrix diagram is shown in Table 10. Note that for each of the teacher functions, the department instructors assume primary, secondary, or no responsibility. With such an analysis, job descriptions are established to reflect the new responsibilities as identified by department teachers using consensus-reaching techniques.

Teacher Functions	Teacher A	Teacher B	Teacher C	Teacher D	Teacher E
Designing Curriculum	◉	▲	◯	◯	▲
Using Technology	▲	▲	◉	◯	◯
Department Management (Team Leader)	◯	◉	▲	◯	▲
Lecturing/ Presenting	◯	▲	◯	◉	▲
Group Facilitation	◯	◉	◯	▲	◯
Research and Development	◯	◯	▲	▲	◉
Evaluation	◯	◯	◯	▲	◉

KEY

◉ Primary Responsibility

◯ Secondary Responsibility

▲ Little or No Responsibility

Table 10—Functional Analysis Matrix Diagram

Such a team-planned system requires a change in thinking about teaching accountability from the usual factors such as student/teacher ratios, class sizes, and student contact hours. With these new systems of team planning and delivery, other criteria need to be established to measure instructional effectiveness and accountability. TQI offers the tools, techniques, and concepts to make this happen.

Customer Service

The customer service approaches should not compel instructors to abdicate any of their responsibilities. The teacher continues to have responsibility to examine the needs of students as well as other stakeholders, as they make curriculum decisions using their past educational preparation and experience. Students may assist in the design of learning requirements and classroom management procedures, however, the final rules and regulations are decided upon and used by teachers. The teacher also maintains responsibility for assessment processes including the evaluation of students.

These responsibilities can best be carried out with effective communication between faculty and students. Discussions occur regarding examinations, grading, student and faculty expectations, and guidelines for attendance, assignments, and participation, then, the final decisions are made by the teacher after weighing student input.

TQI provides the framework for teachers to address many other classroom issues. While many of the skills, techniques, and tools being advanced under the framework of quality have been used for years by many teachers, the language may be strange and some of the strategies may be different. Because the basic concepts were used by many in the past, they are not usually opposed, once understood by all concerned.

Teachers soon come to realize that TQI is based on sound theories of leadership, planning, and evaluation and there is an emphasis placed on the dignity and worth of individuals. Instructors are the ones most able to affect changes needed in their institution. Good leadership, careful planning, intensive training, and modeling by administrators will help convince teachers that TQI offers many benefits for them and their students.

In the classroom, instructors function much like managers of a business. While there may be some constraints, teachers usually have the freedom to make changes. This freedom to act is central to the TQI concept and application in the classroom is possible and even attractive to some instructors.

While teachers think of students as customers, that view is not universal. It is often resisted and even resented by some. One reason is that the customer service focus in education seems to be too narrow. Students are not customers in the same sense as manufacturing and service organizations have customers. In those settings the customer is always assumed to be right and that assumption may not fit in education. However, the instructor should examine the needs and expectations of student customers and review the needs of other stakeholders in the teaching/learning process.

Viewing students as customers may require teachers to look at things differently. It involves a student-centered approach. Much more research is conducted and more data is analyzed as the need for more relevant and timely information about students becomes apparent. Data gathered includes both information about past learning experiences and more current information about student experiences and test results.

In the pages which follow, some helpful tips and examples are provided to assist instructors as they examine how these approaches might be used in their own teaching environment. They are grouped in the following four categories.

- TQI in Curriculum Design

- Classroom Management

- Changes in Teaching and Instructional Environment

- TQI in Assessment Processes

TQI IN CURRICULUM DESIGN

The design of instructional material offers many opportunities for faculty to use total quality improvement concepts, tools, and techniques. The goal, to design and organize curriculum, teaching, assessment, and advancement of students around successful learning activities, is not different from traditional competency-based curriculum design. Faculty carefully define what is meant by *successful learning* in clear, measurable terms. The best indication that learning has occurred is the mastery of outcomes. Instruction is delivered in small, integrated units. This enhances the self-esteem of students who experience success in small increments.

As instructional materials are prepared, a set of quality standards is used. They are developed by instructional teams with input from an instructor focus group. A customer service emphasis is incorporated into the design of the materials, together with the Plan-Do-Check-Act (PDCA) approach and problem-solving activities for students. The goal is to set up processes to be sure that continuous improvement is built into the design and redesign of instructional materials.

Using multiple approaches to teaching, a single-textbook approach is replaced by a broad based, flexible, and focused curriculum which is based on individual differences of students. This individualized philosophy is reflected in the types of instructional materials designed and used.

In this approach, time-honored practices of bell-curved evaluation and grading distributions are abandoned in favor of criterion-referenced systems. Calendar-based, time-referenced scheduling also comes under review. Concepts such as mastery learning, competency-based curriculum, and outcome-based education demand that performance standards be set for students.

CLASSROOM MANAGEMENT AND TEACHING APPLICATIONS

To avoid wasting students' time, every class should begin on time. As students realize that instruction will always start on time, they will also arrive on schedule. Students have a right to expect that they will receive instruction during times listed in the course syllabus and this requires careful planning by the instructor and general agreement by all that starting and ending classes on schedule is important.

Classroom management applications result in agreements between students and the teachers about attendance and the completion of homework assignments. Just as the teacher has the responsibility to start and end classes on time, the student should agree to attend classes regularly and complete all assignments.

Students should be aware of teacher expectations and course objectives. Before the course content is presented, a course syllabus listing objectives, resources, and learning activities provided for students will be helpful and serve that purpose.

A set of written guidelines will ensure that expectations are clear to all. The development of these guidelines provides a good opportunity for the teacher to use quality and consensus-reaching tools.

Prerequisites

Some people believe that an open door policy means every student has a right to enroll in any course he/she wants. This notion that *everyone should have an opportunity to fail*, does not fit the TQI concept. As a part of the quality process, instructors counsel students and ensure that they have mastered prerequisites before enrolling in advanced courses. This compels the institution to have a strong developmental program to help students attain skills necessary to be successful.

Another feature of quality relates to testing. Examinations should be based on the learning objectives and free from surprise and trick questions. Students should know the grade value placed on each test and instructors should try to relieve the students of stress created by examinations.

CHANGES IN TEACHING AND
THE INSTRUCTIONAL ENVIRONMENT

Besides the team planning and decision making to determine responsibilities, changes occur in the classroom and laboratory environments. A positive, supportive environment to encourage learners to accept more responsibility and become self-directed is advocated. This may be happening now in some schools, however, it is usually occurring in isolated programs.

Many believe that the teaching environment will positively influence student performance. A sound TQI environment such as described below will significantly increase learning.

Use of Affective Techniques

There are several other techniques which foster affective approaches to teaching. Many have proven to be very effective. A teacher responding with kindness and empathy, facilitating good human relationships among students, giving personal attention, and recognizing individual students as being valued and cared for can have a profound influence.

One program which has attained national attention is the AS ALTA Success Formula program which focuses on increasing student persistence based on the student's own motivation/desire to succeed. Designed by Dr. Edward "Chip" Anderson, professor in the UCLA Graduate School of Education, the formula includes the establishment of major experiences which impact on the student's desire to persist. Anderson contends that these *Big Arrow* experiences can be either positive or negative based on the provider's application. Global in nature, the AS ALTA Success Formula is a systematic approach to improving the human development aspects of instruction.[15]

This human development aspect was also documented during a study conducted at Fox Valley Technical College. A structured curriculum design approach called DACUM was used to establish a set of competencies for instructors. What evolved was a comprehensive list of preferred teacher characteristics which are grouped under five separate categories of relationships as shown in Table 11.

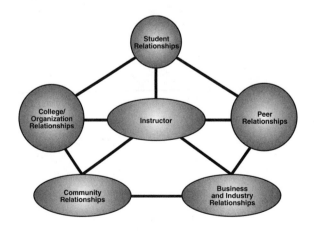

Table 11—DACUM Competencies of Effective Teaching

Accelerated Learning Systems

An approach aimed at improving *cycle time*, by increasing the speed and changing the method in which students learn is called *accelerated learning*. Lakeshore Technical College in Wisconsin and Maricopa Community College in Arizona have piloted these new systems. Students become directly involved in their own learning activities. Different learning modules are used simultaneously in a laboratory setting as students proceed at a pace consistent with their unique talents, experiences, and abilities. Similar to individualized instructional approaches popular in the 1970s, these student-centered systems foster self-directed growth using new discoveries about how the brain works. This learning management system compels students to identify then develop their own personal learning style.

Colin Rose, an advocate of accelerated learning, contends that everything in the learning environment, including color, sound, texture, rhythm, shapes, and even the appearance of the instructional materials is important as an influence of learning.[16] While many examples of these environmental influences are usually from the elementary grades, an increasing number of secondary teachers and professors in colleges and universities are changing the environment in which they teach and experiencing positive results.

The teacher serves as the learning facilitator who guides students based on each individual's learning style. Expected learning outcomes are detailed and resources are suggested to complement those selected by students. The traditional classroom environment evolves to become a learning center. According to Colin Rose, the primary features of accelerated learning systems are as follows:

- Learning outcomes are clearly defined and measurable.

- Multiple resources are available to support those selected by students.

- Limited large-group activities are replaced by student teams and individualized activities.

- Mastery of learning objectives determines the length of courses.

- Teachers become facilitators, coaches, diagnosticians.

- Multiple courses are offered simultaneously in the same laboratory.

- Emphasis is placed on learning to learn and enjoying learning.

- Emerging technologies are used creatively in the teaching/learning process.

- Problem-solving and team development is fostered.

- Learning areas are attractive, comfortable, productive centers.[17]

These new approaches are based on proven learning theories which recognize that people learn in different ways. Emphasis is on experiential learning because proponents believe that students learn best by doing. Students take responsibility for determining their optimal learning style and selecting their learning resources. Time-honored traditions related to student time requirements and teacher roles are challenged and traditional norm-referenced grading is replaced by mastery learning systems. This *success for all students* concept is based on theories advocated years ago by Benjamin Bloom. There is the realization that anyone can learn how to learn faster, easier, and better and this builds student self esteem and confidence as they achieve success and respond creatively to new information and ideas. The teacher orchestrates the processes using carefully designed instructional materials which detail learning objectives and suggest activities and resources for students. The goal is to have every student master all learning objectives.

The Teaching Laboratory Approach

The Graduate School of Business at the University of Chicago uses a unique activity to improve teaching, curriculum, or research called the *Teaching Laboratory*, the idea originated from a student suggestion. Its strength is the direct involvement of teams of graduate students to improve existing courses or design new ones. According to Harry Roberts (Chicago TQM Conference, April, 1993), the *Teaching Laboratory* has been successful. With respect to on-going courses, the students develop feedback mechanisms that tell the instructor continually and quickly what is and what is not working. Other tools are used, such as focus groups and video taping, but the key tool is a simple fast-feedback questionnaire used at almost all class sessions. Students are also involved in curriculum development, including the design of proposals for new courses. Students benchmark techniques employed in businesses to ensure that general management courses are relevant.[18]

Guaranteeing TQI Competencies for Graduates

Perhaps the best way to ensure that TQI concepts, techniques, and tools are used in the teaching/learning process is to provide assurances that graduates will possess a set of TQI competencies to take with them to their next experience in education or the workplace. Such a plan must be developed in cooperation with the instructors, after they have had training in TQI.

Fox Valley Technical College established such a plan in 1991. A team commissioned by the college president used several focus groups of teachers to come up with a set of measurable competencies for all graduates. The competencies were grouped in five main clusters as follows:

- Continuous Improvement in a Global Context

- Process Improvement

- Teamwork

- Customer Focus

- Problem Solving

Once the competencies were agreed upon, a plan was established to integrate them into the College curriculum. It was decided that the competencies will be taught at three levels: awareness, application, and integration.

The awareness level is provided through the regular general studies courses. At this level, students learn the quality improvement process tools and techniques and are given a basic awareness and understanding of the competencies to be mastered before graduation. For example, the mathematics department courses provide instruction in the competencies related to statistical process control and other tool applications. The English department instructors teach teamwork and team building techniques and the behavioral science courses contain instruction in conflict resolution and consensus-reaching skills. Since all college students are required to take general studies classes, they gain awareness of the TQI competencies needed for graduation.

The application level is taught in the 62 instructional programs. Instructors from each of those programs meet in teams and design matrix diagrams to detail the application of TQI competencies in the various courses of the program. Instructors accept the responsibility to ensure that the competencies are applied in the appropriate program courses.

In the integration level, program instructors plan culminating experiences for their students to ensure that the competency clusters are learned by all graduates. Each program area selects projects, internships, or research activities for their students to complete before graduation.

This model, shown in Table 12, seems to work well. Instructors are given assistance in the curriculum revisions needed through the assignment of curriculum facilitators to each program area.

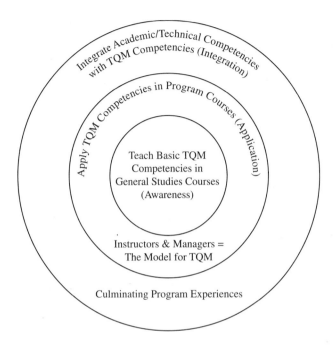

Integrate Academic/Technical Competencies with TQM Competencies (Integration)

Apply TQM Competencies in Program Courses (Application)

Teach Basic TQM Competencies in General Studies Courses (Awareness)

Instructors & Managers = The Model for TQM

Culminating Program Experiences

Table 12—Integration Model—TQI Competencies for Graduates

Such a system will provide employers with graduates ready to work in the world of quality. The Fox Valley plan guarantees employers that graduates possess these competencies. The guarantee provides that if the graduates do not have competence in each of the stated clusters, they will be retrained in total quality at no cost.

TQI IN THE ASSESSMENT PROCESS

Classroom assessment is used to systematically determine how well instruction is meeting the needs of students. It addresses continuous improvement by providing a constant quality check on learning outcomes. Assessment data is shared with students who become partners in the teaching/learning process. Following are some examples of different techniques for classroom assessment.

The Minute Paper

The minute paper is a quick way to get student feedback on a unit or activity. At the end of a unit or classroom activity, the teacher asks students to state, in writing, the most important thing they have learned and also write what is still unclear. Students are given one minute to respond. All responses are reviewed by the teacher to capture the general feeling of students about the session. Feedback is given to students at the next class period. This simple assessment tool, advocated by Dr. Patricia Cross, is a powerful way for a teacher to get immediate feedback in a quick, nonthreatening way.[19]

Chain Notes

Chain notes help teachers find out how students are responding to the work of the class at any given moment. A large envelope displaying one question about the class is circulated and as the envelope reaches each student, he/she responds by writing and inserting a note in the envelope. Similar to the minute paper, chain notes give the teacher information about the value of the class to the students. The question may refer to a specific topic which was covered, a resource which was used, or an assignment which was given.

Plus/Delta

A flipchart or blackboard is needed when using the Plus/Delta tool to capture feedback about the strengths and weaknesses of an activity. Two columns are drawn—one with the plus sign ($+$) as a header and the other with a delta sign (Δ). The teacher asks for spontaneous responses to the question: "What went well in this unit?" and records comments in the *plus* column. After those responses are recorded, the teacher asks the second question: "What could be improved the next time this unit is studied?" Those responses are recorded in the *delta* column. Feedback is analyzed for patterns and used to review material or improve the teaching/learning process the next time the unit is presented. Because input is gathered in an interactive classroom setting, students may be influenced by one another's comments.

Course Survey Evaluations

Evaluations using a survey instrument are commonly used to improve teaching. These questionnaires may be especially effective if certain precautions are taken. At the University of Chicago, the Graduate School of Business faculty all use the same instrument (Fast-Feedback Questionnaire) with systematic public reporting of the results.[20] At Fox Valley Technical College, students complete an evaluation survey once during each course offering. The teacher shares the feedback with the dean or team leader of the department and an action plan is prepared if the information gathered warrants. Its main purpose is to systematically gather information to foster continuous improvement. With this in mind, instructors must be involved in selecting the survey form and establishing the guidelines for its use.

Focus Groups

Focus groups are used to gather information from a group of students on a particular issue. An overview of the topic or issue is given and responses are solicited using a structured approach. Ground rules for the group discussion are followed and all responses are considered to be okay. A specific time period is used (an hour seems to work best). The participants are selected randomly and all are encouraged to participate. A moderator and recorder are used to gather the information about a new initiative or activity being proposed or a particular problem. At Fox Valley Technical College, focus groups are used regularly and one such group assisted in the design of a point-of-service *report card* system now used in service departments throughout the College. The system is based on the premise that students like to grade service in the same way they are evaluated. Table 13 shows the report card they designed.

Student Services Report Card...Give Us a Grade!						

We would like to know what you think of the service you just received. What grade would you give us (circle grade).

						Comments/Suggestions
Knowledgeable staff	A	B	C	D	F	_____
Friendly and helpful staff	A	B	C	D	F	_____
Prompt service	A	B	C	D	F	_____
Easy-to-follow and logical forms	A	B	C	D	F	_____
Availability of printed materials and brochures	A	B	C	D	F	_____
Service environment	A	B	C	D	F	_____
Convenient office hours	A	B	C	D	F	_____
Overall service to you	A	B	C	D	F	_____

Date: _____   Time of Day: _____

Thanks! Please deposit in any suggestion box on campus.

Table 13—Point-of-Service Report Card

Student Needs Survey

The Needs Survey is used to find out what students need and want. A special instrument is designed based on the type of information requested. For example, one may be designed to find out interest in a particular course, workshop, or service or one may be used to solicit opinions about an initiative being considered. The instrument contains a series of statements and the student rates the relative importance on a scale. Decisions are made using the results of the survey.

SUMMARY COMMENTS

1. Since the instructor controls the methods, processes, and environment in which learning occurs, any changes require his/her full support. Mandated changes won't work.

2. The TQI training program for teachers should provide a set of tools to select from as they decide exactly how to facilitate TQI into the learning environment of their classrooms.

3. There is no one right method of teaching. Several factors impact on learning success and often they are beyond the teacher's control.

4. Major improvement in education will not occur without the support and cooperation of the teaching staff.

5. One of the long-range goals of a school which implements TQI should be to graduate students who possess TQI competencies.

6. Teachers need support and training to enable them to integrate TQI into the teaching/learning process.

7. Quality tools and techniques can be effectively applied in all aspects of instruction including curriculum design, classroom management, teaching, evaluation, and assessment.

Chapter 5
Community Service—
New Role for Education

Education contributes greatly to the economy of the region. Graduates add value with the special talents and knowledge they bring to employers. Research, consulting, and expertise provided by administrators, teachers, and staff benefit the agencies and businesses of the community. New businesses are often attracted to a region because of the quality of its educational programs. The cultural, intellectual, leadership, and civic contributions provided by faculty, staff, and students are invaluable to most communities.

Likewise, the community contributes greatly to education. Many educational institutions could not survive without financial assistance provided through scholarships, endowments, and donations. People from the community serve as volunteers or adjunct faculty for the educational institutions in their region. They bring a special expertise to education, especially as teacher aides in elementary schools and as instructors in professional and technical courses offered in colleges and universities. Citizens help in many other ways by serving on boards, advisory committees, and fund-raising groups. With this support, partnerships developed between educators and their communities are usually mutually beneficial.

Some colleges and universities have discovered another important niche in community services. This new role is to provide, under contract, customized training and technical assistance. Community colleges, in particular, have expanded their missions to include this new and expanding market. The internal implementation of Total Quality Improvement (TQI) has often enhanced this service effort and given colleges and universities new opportunities and greater credibility in their service areas.

As educational institutions initiate quality processes internally, the business world has taken notice. TQI is a private sector system, born and raised in the manufacturing and service world. It is natural that the business sector would be pleased to see educators try their practices.

TQI has also provided the tools and techniques to assist educators in designing and assessing its community service mission. Quality implementation provides the planning tools and strategies for college departments to establish their mission statements and strategic directions to assist business and industry. The tools are also used to evaluate the effectiveness of the service and instruction provided.

Employers soon recognize that service and instruction from schools pays off by providing a well-trained work force to give them the edge over their competitors. Foreign businesses have learned that their employees are their most important resource. The Japanese especially have proven that employee education and training pays dividends in terms of greater productivity and increased market share. They have learned that by reordering their organizational structures and establishing new work systems, they can empower frontline employees to make the changes necessary to produce quality in products and services.

This philosophy of staff development and training is now being adopted by American businesses and industries. While training is costly, progressive organizations have found that an investment in people leads to better products and services produced at reduced costs. Many of these organizations are turning to educational institutions for training and other assistance.

Through this assistance, educators assume a leadership role in improving the economy of the region. As the academic and cultural center of the community, an educational institution is enhanced by support from the community.

One important way to provide leadership and assistance is to set up programs offering training in quality improvement for the community. As an educational institution implements total quality internally, it will discover that it has a vast array of new quality improvement programs which it can share.

Some schools decide to serve as the catalyst to promote total quality improvement in their region. They establish quality resource centers for use by organizations and individuals interested in continuous improvement. They also set up quality networks to provide sharing opportunities for quality proponents.

An excellent example of a quality network is the Madison Area Quality Improvement Network (MAQIN), located in Madison, Wisconsin. MAQIN serves hundreds of organizations and agencies by providing resources, training, and programs to members. A nonprofit organization not affiliated to any educational institution, MAQIN serves as a coordinating agency. It hosts regular programs conducted by local organizations willing to share the trials, tribulations, successes, and innovations resulting from TQI implementation. Workshops and programs feature TQI experts from around the Country. The annual Hunter Quality Conference attracts hundreds of registrants from this Country and abroad. There are several networks and quality resource centers affiliated with educational institutions.

An example of an exemplary center is one located at Fox Valley Technical College. The College used the quality process it implemented internally as the model for designing and implementing its community service program. It gained national prominence in the late 1980s and early 1990s when Fox Valley Technical College received several national awards for efforts in implementing quality and establishing an exemplary community service program. Community service awards were given by the American Society for Training and Development (ASTD), IBM Corporation, and the American Association for Community Colleges (AACC).

In 1992, the College received state and national attention for providing customized training and technical assistance programs to over 800 organizations. College staff wrote more than 3,300 training contracts and provided instruction to over 30,000 employees. The College had become involved in many other activities related to economic development in the region.

USING THE QUALITY PROCESS TO ESTABLISH
AND MAINTAIN A COMMUNITY SERVICE PROGRAM

The TQI process was used to prepare the community service mission and set up the organization to deliver the services and instruction. A task force of business, government, education, and public service representatives planned and wrote the mission statement for the new thrust. A subgroup prepared a set of organizational procedures and policies called, *Economic Development Guidelines*. These guidelines were adopted by the College Board of Trustees during the early stages of the quality improvement initiative.[21]

A separate administrative division, Community Relations, was created to spearhead the new initiative and an integrated model was created as the delivery system. This model directed the existing instructional divisions to design and deliver customized educational programs and services. This integrated model was successful because the responsibility was shared and regular faculty and staff accepted this broadened mission. The typical continuing education model used in most colleges places the responsibility for community service programs in a department separate from regular instructional departments. The Fox Valley task force argued that such a *separate division* approach creates competition within the College and confusion for the customer who must deal with different departments depending on the type of service desired. The advantage they saw in keeping the responsibility in the regular departments of the College was that the faculty and staff would remain current and this would be reflected in their curriculum.

COMMUNITY SERVICE CUSTOMERS

Once the mission statement was in place and the organizational structure decided upon, the next step was to define customers and determine their needs. After considerable deliberation the following customers were defined:

- Corporate Businesses and Industries

- Small Businesses (less than 50 employees)

- Community Agencies (public and private)

- Organized Labor (construction and industrial)

- Farmers and Agri-Businesses

- Other Educational Institutions in the Region

After the customers were defined, the next step was to determine their specific needs and expectations. Focus groups were established and surveys were conducted and the following services and programs were identified:

- Customized Training and Retraining Programs

- Technical Assistance Programs and Services

- Technology Transfer Programs and Services

- Industrial Testing Services

- Computer Resource Centers for Software and Equipment Selection

- Training Facilities Specific to Business and Industry

- Grant Writing/Funding Assistance

- Career Development and Placement Services

- Industrial Development and Recruitment of New Business and Industry

After the programs and services were determined, the next step was to set up the system for delivery to the customer groups. Several college teams were set up and the administrators accepted the challenge to make it work.

The major shift was that the college became a proactive promoter of customized instruction, technical assistance, and other services. The college aggressively marketed the programs and services to the private sector and the thrust gained momentum. Soon, college-wide involvement in community relations intensified beyond expectations. College executives and staff became active in economic development agencies and faculty and staff were given incentives to participate with local service organizations. Instructors and others were given support to participate with national and international groups of all types.

Quality process methods and tools were used to organize and foster this effort. Permanent focus groups were organized to monitor plans and recommend new initiatives for their customer group. Table 14 shows the permanent focus groups which were established.

COMMUNITY SERVICE/CUSTOMER SERVICE	
Customer	**Focus Group Organization**
Corporate Businesses/Industries	Corporate Executive Council for Economic Development
Small Businesses	Small Business Advisory Council
Public Agencies/Government	Presidential Luncheon Groups
Farmers and Agri-Businesses	District Agriculture Committee
Organized Labor Groups	Labor Leaders Breakfast Group
K-12 Education Systems	Tech Prep Articulation Committee

Table 14—Permanent Focus Groups Established to Plan and Monitor Programs

Enrollments have grown as employers discover programs and services available. A customer satisfaction plan was adopted and a satisfaction guarantee is given with each written contract. The guarantee provides a refund of the fees if the employer is not fully satisfied with the service.

As the program has grown, several innovative projects evolved. These special features are shown in Table 15.

ECONOMIC DEVELOPMENT MODEL
Special Features
• Technical, Research, Innovation Park (TRI-Park)
• Business Training Centers
• Computer Integrated Manufacturing Network
• Regional/National/International Training Centers at the College
• Quality and Productivity Resource Center
• Quality Improvement Process Specialist Degree Program
• Team Focus™ Planning for Business & Industry
• Fox Valley Quality Academy

Table 15—Innovative Features of the Economic Development Model

TECHNICAL, RESEARCH, INNOVATION PARK (TRI-PARK)

A nonprofit corporation was organized to provide one of the first community college affiliated industrial parks in the Country. This Technical, Research, Innovation Park (TRI-Park) is a joint effort involving the College, county government, area chambers, and the business sector. A set of covenants ensures that the Park meets its objective of recruiting businesses and industries related to programs offered at the College. The covenants require that the park tenants enter into a formal relationship with the College to assist and support its programs and services. For example, students and faculty work together with TRI-Park businesses on projects related to school programs and the businesses involved.

The hub of the TRI-Park is the business training center, the D.J. Bordini Technological Innovation Center. This business-oriented facility was constructed with strong financial support from the community. It has become the formal link to the College's vast network of programs and services as the flexible training and service center is used almost exclusively to provide programs for area businesses. Its resource centers are used extensively by both business people and the faculty and staff of the College. One important resource area is the Fox Valley Quality/Productivity Resource Center (Q/PRC).

QUALITY/PRODUCTIVITY RESOURCE CENTER (Q/PRC)

The Quality/Productivity Resource Center (Q/PRC) was established by a group of TQI practitioners representing a cross section of business, industry, government, and education. The group serves as the advisory board for quality and productivity in the region. The mission statement of the Q/PRC is as follows:

> *The Quality/Productivity Resource Center (Q/PRC) is an organized effort coordinated by local business and industry and Fox Valley Technical College to assist local business, industry, and nonprofit organizations in their efforts to improve quality and productivity.*

Organizations of any size and type (private, public, manufacturing, service, retail, government, and education) are encouraged to join. An annual membership fee is paid and a contact person from the member organization is responsible for disseminating information about the center to the other employees. Individual memberships are available. The Q/PRC is organized as an entity of the college foundation which provides the staff and resources for the center.

A newsletter is published quarterly, highlighting quality and productivity instructional programs sponsored by the Q/PRC. Resources and services, including computer data searches on special topics and resources, are available to members.

Members automatically become a part of the Fox Valley Quality Network which meets monthly. The network brings *state-of-the-art* information to assist organizations in developing and improving total quality improvement processes. Programs featuring local member organizations are conducted to share experiences, successes, and challenges. The network becomes a forum for organizations with specific needs.

Today, almost 200 organizations are members of the Fox Valley Quality/Productivity Resource Center recently renamed the Performance Excellence Alliance. It has one of the most extensive quality resource collections in the Country and sponsors outstanding programs for business and industry, bringing experts to the region including Stephen Covey, Joel Barker, Margaret Wheatley, and Peter Senge.

COLLEGE ENTREPRENEURIAL BUSINESSES

Another benefit of the college community service program is the entrepreneurial businesses which evolved. These self-supporting profit centers contribute to regional economic development and assist the College by providing finances for operations. Enterprise centers are linked to training activities in college specialty areas. The Flexography Technical Center, for example, evolved as a provider of training and research services for the graphic arts industry. In 1992, an Italian manufacturer donated a three-color flexographic press valued at over $675,000. Other vendors followed with equipment donations and endowments and today most of the equipment is provided to the Center at no cost.

Another successful enterprise is the Fox Valley Computer Integrated Manufacturing Network. A cross-functional team of instructors and their managers designed a network linking the campus departments in a simulated Computer Automated Manufacturing (CAM) operation. Products are produced on the network while students and instructors demonstrate the concepts to business and industry who wish to automate. The system features computerized order entry, Computer Aided Design (CAD), automated graphics display, numerically controlled machine tool center, and a robotics manufacturing cell. The network team designed this nonprofit business which conducts actual operations and simulates larger systems.

NATIONAL QUALITY ACADEMY

Perhaps the most significant business venture that the College became involved in is the National Quality Academy (NQA). This college enterprise business was acquired from the College in 1993, by Noel-Levitz Centers, Inc., the Country's largest consulting group for higher education. Formed as an affiliate of the College, the National Quality Academy and its forerunner, the Fox Valley Technical College Quality Academy, provide products and services to clients from business and industry and other educational institutions implementing total quality improvement. Thousands of students and practitioners have benefited from consulting services and training programs conducted both at the College and on site.

Over 300 educational institutions and more than 60 local businesses have participated in Academy programs. Educators from all over the United States and from Australia, Brazil, Mexico, New Zealand, Costa Rica, El Salvador, Netherlands, Denmark, United Kingdom, Sweden, Bermuda, Newfoundland, Palau, Saipan, Taiwan, British Columbia, Alberta, and Ontario have participated in the training and services provided. Several Regional Quality Academies are affiliates to NQA as the total quality improvement effort expands. In April, 1995, USA Group acquired both Noel-Levitz and the National Quality Academy.

The Fox Valley Technical College Quality Academy serves the College service area. An IBM software package, Team Focus™ is available to companies as a part of their planning and priority setting process. An annual Quality Commitment Day continues to be held. National TQI experts present their theories and ideas to college employees and people from business and industry. At the same time, the college celebrates its successes in continuous quality improvement.

In all, sixteen entrepreneurial businesses and several customized programs were established through the creativity of the faculty and staff of the College. Through unique relationships established with equipment vendors, College businesses and programs have been established to serve the industries and the college itself. An indirect benefit is the influx of thousands of trainers who travel to Fox Valley from around the world to participate in these programs and services. Enrollments in these unique programs have come from all fifty states and eighteen foreign countries. The economic benefit to the region has been enormous.

BENEFITS OF COMMUNITY SERVICE PROGRAMS

There are many reasons why colleges and universities may want to implement similar programs and services for business and industry. The most compelling reason is to assist business to be competitive with those from other countries. Competitive advantage involves having a well trained and educated work force. This is difficult because most of the people who will be working in business and industry in the year 2000 are already employed. This means that there is a gigantic task of educating millions of people currently employed. Advanced technology and new requirements demand that public education become involved, for it is not always possible for business and industry to develop and educate its own employees. If for no other reason than to help this country maintain economic stability, educators must become involved in community partnerships and establish training and education programs for business and industry.

Another important reason to offer these programs is the financial benefits which result. Business and industry is more willing to provide financial assistance to educational institutions when they receive credible programs in return. People from the business world will also participate as resource people, serving on focus groups and advisory committees. Organizations receiving these customized services are usually more willing to donate equipment and scholarships to the FVTC Foundation.

Perhaps the most important reason relates to relevancy. These community service programs keep regular instructional programs current. By articulating with the private sector on a regular basis, faculty remain updated and maintain relevant instructional materials.

SUMMARY COMMENTS

1. Educational institutions should establish strong community articulation programs, including instruction and service for the adults in the communities they serve. Providing customized training to keep the employed updated is an especially important way to enhance the economy.

2. An integrated community service system which includes full-time faculty from regular instructional programs of the college teaching in business and industry, is preferred because of the paybacks to the institution, especially the benefits to teachers and their programs.

3. Community service business enterprises are mutually beneficial because these collaborative activities ensure that the courses for students will be current and provide real-life experiences. At the same time, the enterprises provide vital services to their customers and needed resources to the educational institution.

4. Programs to reeducate the work force require new and flexible delivery systems, often uncommon in higher education. The need is so critical that public education is compelled to participate to keep our economy strong and their instruction relevant.

5. Total quality improvement training and services propels the educational institution into a leadership role as it assists organizations and individuals interested in learning more continuous quality improvement tools and techniques.

Chapter 6
Assessment and Results

Assessment in the TQI process shifts from inspection to prevention as systems and processes are established to prevent problems from occurring later. With this change in emphasis, assessment shifts from singular outcome-based evaluation methods to comprehensive feedback and measurement systems which lead to continuous process improvement. The emphasis is on institutional effectiveness based on student-centered approaches, as reflected in the mission of the institution.

This mission-based approach reflects the character and uniqueness of the institution. It also represents a shift from informal assessment measures to formal approaches which are more comprehensive and systematic. The preferred system is a research design with numerous measures and appropriate process benchmarks to help target the assessment process toward mission-centered criteria and locally established quality standards.

These criteria are different for individual K-12 schools, community colleges, technical institutes, four-year colleges, and universities. Even within each of these educational systems, criteria may be different, making comparisons difficult and inappropriate.

As each institution develops its assessment plan and criteria for measurement, the goal is to determine its level of effectiveness based on the various elements of its mission. This requires identifying customers and stakeholders served, obtaining feedback as to their needs and expectations, and establishing measurement criteria to determine how well those needs and expectations are met. This centers on continuous improvement rather than on snapshot inspections. The measures used are established accordingly.

Since mission statements are vital to the planned success of an organization, they must be specific and up-to-date. The mission sets the direction for the institution and becomes the cornerstone upon which department mission statements evolve. It becomes the official policy of the institution and needs to be reviewed continually by stakeholders to reach broad-based consensus. Such consensus can best be attained using some of the basic TQI planning tools and processes.

Once adopted, the mission statement becomes the basis upon which operational plans are developed and resources are allocated. It is the heart of the assessment program, as emphasis shifts away from traditional process measures such as those used by accreditation agencies. Faculty credentials, learning resource collections, facilities, curriculum materials, and financial resources are still important, however, the main focus is on outcome measures and results rather than cosmetic things. Assessment involves the systematic gathering of information using several measures with the goal of monitoring the effectiveness of the institution as a whole.

Properly selected and used, these measures with an emphasis on self-analysis and improvement are similar in scope to accreditation and reaccreditation studies. With this type of institutional effectiveness approach, crash programs and ad hoc committees to prepare self studies and accreditation reports become unnecessary.

Because this assessment system should foster continuous improvement in teaching, learning, administration, and service, each measurement segment should be selected based on the benefits received through its use. The purpose is to collect information for use in continuous improvement and decision making. To be effective, the measurement focus must move away from micro comparisons and rankings—they are unimportant in a TQI institution.

AN INSTITUTIONAL EFFECTIVENESS AND ASSESSMENT MODEL

There are several good examples of assessment plans for educational institutions. A model, suggested by USA Group National Quality Academy and shown in Table 16, is an upgraded version of the one used for several years at Fox Valley Technical College.

Table 16—Assessment Model

In the model, each measurement is described with a timetable for its use. The influence of continuous quality improvement is fostered with these multiple measures based on the institutional mission and a set of quality standards designed with the help of stakeholders.

These quality standards are established for each of the major functions in administration, operations, and instruction. They reflect what's new and changing, thereby promoting continuous process improvement. Sets of standards may be developed for example, to evaluate teaching, management, use of technology, curriculum design, customer service, communication, and so on. These standards serve as benchmarks during the assessment process and become determinants of the school's success. The results become barometers to monitor continuous improvement.

There are several beliefs underlying the measurement processes of this model:

1. Quality and productivity methods can be just as useful in improving education, as they are in improving a company that produces a product.

2. Personnel in an educational institution, with help from customers and stakeholders, can identify standards for institutional measurement and decision making.

3. Emphasis in this system of assessment should be placed on the improvement of processes in both instruction and service. This leads to better teaching and service and greater student achievement.

4. The problem-solving strategies used require effective application of scientific methodologies and statistical approaches with the use of the Plan-Do-Check-Act (PDCA) cycle.

5. Management, technical, and instructional processes and transactions should be continually reviewed and analyzed with the goal being to achieve excellence.

6. Measurement and analysis should be comprehensive, ongoing, and structured in systematic ways to detect special causes and reduce common cause variability.

7. The organizational climate, appropriately measured, is a good barometer of student and employee satisfaction, management effectiveness, and the overall morale of the college.

8. With fewer mistakes, less rework, fewer delays and snags, continuous review of processes and increased customer satisfaction, college costs will be reduced.

MEASUREMENT COMPONENTS

The measurement vehicles should be selected after the mission statement is in place and following a determination of the quality standards. The institutional effectiveness model which evolves has sets of measures to determine whether there is continuous improvement in instruction, services, and administration. Tools and strategies are used to gather information from all stakeholders.

The model proposed by USA Group National Quality Academy has eleven sets of information gathered regularly to determine institutional effectiveness. These are briefly summarized below.

Organizational Climate

The general climate and morale of the institution is important and should be measured regularly to determine if the key indicators are showing improvement. Human resource management, together with administrative support and effectiveness, are important considerations when analyzing climate. The best way to gather data about these things is to survey employees. The data compared over time will determine if progress is being made. Information, sorted by departments and by personnel levels, will determine if there are differences. The administration, faculty, and staff through this type of survey can assess things such as morale, leadership, peer support, general organizational climate, and several other factors related to quality improvement.

One instrument which may be used is *Organizational Surveys* developed by Likert Associates. This tool produces comparative scores in 34 different categories related to organizational climate.[22] The instrument was first used at Fox Valley in 1986, it was administered annually five times. An analysis of the data prior to 1993 showed that since TQI was implemented there was marked improvement in 25 categories, with 16 of those categories showing improvement at the .01 significance level. The results, compiled and reported on an institution-wide basis and for each manager and administrator, provided a yearly report which compared unit or department ratings with the overall College data. This personalized and confidential information was not circulated throughout the College, however, each manager shared the data with his/her staff and together they developed an improvement plan for the next year.[23]

Because the survey has not been used extensively by educational institutions, Fox Valley recently used another form geared toward education. USA Group National Quality Academy also has a 50-item survey form based on the Malcolm Baldrige Award Criteria and the Presidential Award for Quality Criteria. This *Campus Quality Survey* ™ is described further in the section of this chapter titled *Measuring Total Quality Improvement*.

Community Perception Studies

Perception studies are valuable to assess the overall image of the institution in the community. Periodic surveys among district residents are useful to gain information every two or three years. A telephone questionnaire works best with a sample of the population. The results are compiled and reported to the staff and residents. Results are compared with previous surveys to measure improvement.

Regional Needs Studies

Surveys conducted among different demographic and economic groups in the region help determine whether the needs of the various groups are being met. A large service area may be divided into geographic sections for survey purposes to gather valuable data. Information may be obtained from employers, agencies, high school students, and educators from other schools in the region. The data collected is analyzed to assist the administration and board in deciding on new programs, courses, and services for each region of the district.

Satisfaction Guarantees

Several educational institutions are now using customer service guarantees to show that they are serious about improving the quality of services and instruction. Guarantees reinforce the commitment made to quality and show customers that the organization is willing to stand behind the quality of your programs and services. They are very powerful in that they ensure that all processes are constantly reviewed and upgraded to guarantee success. Colleges and universities, when reviewing their commitment to excellence, should consider providing some written satisfaction guarantees for their students and other customers.

There are usually three different types of satisfaction guarantees which are issued. The first type is a guarantee to employers who receive customized training and technical assistance. This guarantee provides assurance that the contracting organization will be completely satisfied with the instruction or service provided. If not, a refund is given or the instruction is repeated at no cost.

The second type of guarantee assures graduates that the stated outcomes of their courses will be met. Graduates receive free course credits and other services if they do not receive employment in their field of study within six months following graduation. This type of guarantee is also provided to transfer students to assure them that their credits will be accepted by other educational institutions.

The third guarantee assures both graduates and their employers that graduates are competent in their field of study and that they possess total quality improvement skills, tools, and techniques. Competency lists are prepared and, if graduates do not have possess those competencies, they are given free instruction in quality improvement courses, workshops, and seminars to ensure that the concepts and skills are learned.

Guarantees such as these are being established in institutions across the Country. They are important indicators of quality since they provide assurances that certain levels of customer satisfaction will be maintained by the institution. They compel the institution to have standards and processes in all areas from recruitment through graduation. Effective enrollment planning processes and satisfaction guarantees are valuable recruitment tools. They will attract more students, and streamline processes internally.

Employer Satisfaction Surveys

Since many graduates go into full-time employment after graduation, it is a good idea to find out how satisfied employees are with the preparation of the graduates they hire. Using a survey form, employers rate their level of satisfaction with the academic, technical, and affective competencies of graduates. Data is compiled and reported on an institutional level and is also made available to faculty and staff at each program or work unit level. This information is useful to determine the relevancy of the curriculum in both technical and professional programs. The surveys also inform employers that the organization cares about the competence of its graduates.

Graduate Follow Up Studies

Surveys of graduates help to determine how satisfied former students are with the instruction and services they received. They provide valuable information about the current status of graduates as information about types of occupations, salary levels, promotions, and type of work is gathered. Colleges in the Wisconsin Technical College system survey graduates six months following graduation to determine employment status, compensation levels, and other factors. The data is compiled and reported by college and program area. This information is also published and distributed to potential students. On-going surveys are conducted every three to five years in Wisconsin to note further progress of graduates.

Cost Containment Studies

In this era of increasing competition and declining resources, educational institutions are compelled to prepare cost containment plans to project expenditures and revenues and control costs. This type of long-range planning usually covers a three-year period, and the information is updated annually. Budgetary amount and financial goals for programs, personnel, and facilities are established and projections are made for each. Alternative financial projections from various enterprises of the institution are also prepared.

Cost containment plans contain financial containment and reduction targets which are gathered with input from faculty, staff, advisory groups, students, and other stakeholders. Projected revenues and expenditures are included, with the faculty and staff become directly involved in decision making related to financing. Contingency plans developed in advance assist when cuts are required due to unplanned financial limitations.

Student Satisfaction Surveys

There are many ways to get feedback from students. The matrix shown in Table 17 lists several. Through this information, students assess the programs and services they receive. They should have numerous opportunities to evaluate courses they take to ensure that the feedback is reliable and valid. Feedback about both teaching and support services should be gathered regularly. Point-of-service surveys, conducted in various service departments of the institution, provide immediate feedback which is generally very useful to the departments.

	What Do Our Customers Want?	How Satisfied Are Our Customers?	What Is Happening to Our Customers?
One-on-One Interview	⊙	⊙	○
Focus Group	⊙	○	▲
Survey (Phone, Mail, Classroom)	⊙	⊙	⊙
Point-of-Service Evaluation	▲	⊙	▲
Suggestion System	⊙	▲	▲
Observation of Customers	▲	▲	⊙
Records/Database Analysis	○	▲	⊙

KEY

⊙ Very Useful

○ Useful

▲ Less Useful

Table 17—Feedback Methods Matrix Diagram

In addition to surveys, students, employees, and visitors should be able to offer ideas, commend individuals, and voice complaints through a suggestion system. This feedback system is effective if processes are established to collect the suggestions on a regular basis and do something about them.

Input can also be obtained through focus groups. Trained focus group facilitators conduct these sessions to receive input regarding issues or problems on campus from a sample of students or staff. Focus groups can also be used by instructors to gain feedback regarding various aspects of the teaching/learning process.

USA Group Noel-Levitz Centers has designed a *Student Satisfaction Inventory*™ which is unique in several ways. It described later in this chapter, under the section titled, *Measuring Total Quality Improvement*.

External Program and Service Assessments

Reviews of programs and services by parties external to institutions are required to find out how well programs and services are meeting the needs of customers and stakeholders. These program and service audits are similar to reaccreditation reviews as they use external examiners who participate in comprehensive reviews of programs and services using data gathered through surveys and self-analysis.

Individuals with special expertise review survey results, data, and other print information prior to the on-site visit and use quality standards established by the institution to review criteria. The audit process provides valuable information, suggestions, and recommendations for continuous improvement. The departments and programs selected for this extensive review should be selected using established criteria and rotation systems set up by the research department or administration.

Faculty and staff will be willing to cooperate and establish audit processes agreed upon by all parties. Information gathered must be disseminated in ways not threatening to those involved.

Competitive Benchmarking Studies

Competitive benchmarking is the process of reviewing exemplary services and programs of other organizations and using the information to improve your institution. Organizations are selected because of their outstanding programs or services and a team of faculty and staff visit the organization and use carefully designed processes to gather and analyze information.

Several institutions were used by Fox Valley Technical College to benchmark its quality improvement process. As a member of the Continuous Quality Improvement Network (CQIN), a group of community colleges which have implemented TQI, Fox Valley gathers valuable information as it benchmarks other institutions which have excelled in things such as accelerated learning systems, institutional assessment programs, computer integrated manufacturing networks, and leadership and staff development initiatives.

This suggested effectiveness and assessment model is provided to assist others in establishing their own plan. It would be inappropriate for a school to adopt the model in this book without extensive study and review by the faculty and staff from their own institution. The best plan is one designed internally with input from external stakeholders. As institutions design their institutional effectiveness model they should consider these suggestions:

1. The assessment plan should be based on the mission and the strategic directions of the institution.

2. A set of quality standards should be developed with input from managers, faculty, staff, and external stakeholders, including students and employers.

3. Several sets of measures should be included in the information gathering process.

4. The primary focus of it all is on institutional effectiveness through continuous quality improvement.

Measuring Total Quality Improvement

Recently, many educational institutions have attempted to measure the effectiveness of TQI programs they have implemented. Most of these efforts involve one or more survey instruments using a set of criteria as a basis for the measurement. Attempts are also being made to translate the Malcolm Baldrige Examination Criteria to education. In Europe, Canada, Australia, and New Zealand, ISO 9000 Standards are being customized for use in education.

The USA Group National Quality Academy and USA Group Noel-Levitz have each designed survey instruments which show great promise. These instruments measure student and employee satisfaction. Each item on the survey is rated by the respondent to indicate both the level of satisfaction and an opinion about how valuable the service is. A gap analysis statistic which results from these ratings show the difference between the level of satisfaction and the value given for each item.

The *Student Satisfaction Inventory*™ shows the importance student place on various services and their level of satisfaction with them. A summary report provides the institution with valuable information that can be used for planning purposes. Used as one part of the overall assessment plan, this data will provide important information useful for the institution as it continues its quest for quality improvement.

The *Campus Quality* Survey™ designed by USA Group National Quality Academy asks personnel to rate several items based on Malcolm Baldrige and Presidential Quality Award Criteria. Through these ratings, the board and administration can determine how well the employee expectations are being met as reported by the different personnel levels and compared with other similar institutions.

The philosophy underlying this entire assessment process is the focus on continuous improvement. This philosophy reminds us that quality levels reached today won't be good enough tomorrow. Therefore, the standards of excellence and institutional effectiveness should be constantly upgraded.

RESULTS FROM IMPLEMENTING QUALITY IMPROVEMENT

What results can educators expect when implementing TQI? What are the returns on the investment made to create this transformation in the institution? Are the results worth the time and money? These questions and others will come up and need to be answered. There is difficulty in responding to questions such as these because there are no easy answers.

First, the impacts of the quality improvement process aren't quickly apparent. The up-front training is expensive and time consuming and major changes won't happen and positive results won't appear until people have learned to apply the concepts, tools, and techniques of quality. Also, the impacts are very dependent on the leadership provided in the departments. Some managers take more time to support these changes because of the major shift in how things are done. Those departments will be slower to report progress.

Therefore, great patience is needed even though people will be looking for quick results. Top-level commitment is vital. The early expectations of staff create special challenges for leaders which might be hard to overcome.

If there is enough patience, the positive results will begin to justify the early investments in training. The organization will improve and show results in time, if the quality process is properly applied. Improvement will surely occur when administrators, faculty, and support staff work together with other stakeholders to identify requirements, make necessary changes, measure the results, and standardize the changes which show positive benefits. As this is repeated throughout the institution, staff use continuous improvement strategies to eliminate nonconformances. Positive results become more apparent as improvements are made in small increments throughout the college.

The compilation of these benefits from the departments and the positive results documented during the assessment process produce outcomes critics have been asking for. Schools have the responsibility to provide the same kind of information and documented results that corporations provide for their board of directors and stockholders. In education, results should be reviewed in four areas as suggested by these questions:

1. Has learning improved as a result of TQI implementation?

2. Is the institution more efficient?

3. Do the graduates leave with TQI competencies?

4. Has the culture of the institution improved?

These should be the criteria used as the results of TQI are examined. The institutional effectiveness plan must include answers to those questions and the results shown should provide us with enough positive data to justify the quality initiative.

The kinds of results which educational institutions might expect are reflected in an analysis of the major outcomes which occurred, over nine years, at Fox Valley Technical College. Positive outcomes from other institutions also provide insight about the kinds of benefits which might be expected when schools implement TQI.

Has Learning Improved as a Result of TQI Implementation?

Learning improvement is measured by studying the successes of students in courses and by determining whether there is satisfaction among the various stakeholders. Six years into the process, Fox Valley initiated a customer satisfaction guarantee system for students, graduates, employers, and other educational institutions. The guarantees ensure that instruction and services provided meet the needs of students and other stakeholders. There are three guarantees provided:

1. A guarantee that graduates will have success in obtaining employment in job-related occupations.

2. A guarantee that employers will be satisfied with contracted training programs.

3. A guarantee that graduates will have success in transferring credits at other institutions.

An analysis of these guarantees after three years indicates that:

1. From a total of more than 3,000 graduates, only one person asked for free instruction and services because she was unable to obtain a job in her occupational area.

2. During each of the past five years, over 90% of the graduates were placed in jobs related to their educational programs.

3. From more than 3,300 contracts with business, industry, and agencies in 1992-93, only two employers requested a refund because they were not satisfied with the instruction or services.

4. There are written agreements with all of the public universities in Wisconsin to accept a minimum number of credits for those who graduate from Fox Valley. Graduates are able to transfer credits for courses in which they have attained a "C" average or better.

In addition to these positive results because of guarantees, there are other indicators that show there is improved learning. One relates to the declining drop-out rate. The number of persons who withdrew from the college in 1992-93 declined by 32%, according to the annual report prepared by the vice president of academic affairs. He also reported that many students completed their course requirements sooner than the usual time. There are also many reports from faculty about improvements in grade point averages tracked over time.[24]

These positive results are due to many things including major changes in the teaching/learning processes. Some examples of ways to improve learning include:

- The design and use of multiple-course laboratories.

- The use of open-entry/exit enrollment systems.

- Establishment of flexible classes and staff contracts.

- Experimentation with accelerated learning processes.

Faculty throughout the institution are creatively applying TQI principles and tools when designing curriculum, structuring courses, teaching students, and evaluating outcomes.

Employer satisfaction with on-site contract training programs has resulted in tremendous increases in enrollments in customized training and increases in financial and other support from the business community. The two incidences of employer dissatisfaction mentioned earlier were quickly corrected. One complaint was due to an unfortunate comment by the instructor; the other was the result of an inadequate curriculum.

The general satisfaction of employers has resulted in the college receiving national awards as the outstanding community college in providing business/industry customized training and technical assistance. One of these awards was presented at the American Association of Community Colleges National Conference in 1993.

Of special importance are increases in financial assistance from the private sector. There were 22 formal agreements with major vendors for the consignment of new equipment to Fox Valley instructional programs. Local businesses provided much of the funding for two business training centers constructed by the College in two different area industrial parks. According to the foundation director, the College Foundation experienced a 238% increase in cash donations during 1992-93.[25] Several projects created by the college staff in cooperation with area businesses resulted in additional finances to help the College provide quality programs and instruction.

Is The Institution More Efficient?

There are many examples of improved efficiency at Fox Valley Technical College and other colleges which have implemented TQI. They include improvements in service departments as well as increased productivity in the classroom.

Increased efficiencies are the result of basic improvement strategies which include reducing cycle time, simplifying processes, removing or preventing errors, reducing variation, and developing standard processes. It is difficult to measure some of these things and determine the cost savings which are acquired because of the improvements made.

Some areas of improvement reported include:

- Staff reductions due to improved mailroom processes.

- Waiting time reductions by improving the process time in student service areas such admissions, registration, financial aids, veterans benefits, cashier's office, and orientation programs.

- Savings in staff time due to reductions in payroll errors made by staff for part-time faculty and staff.

- Savings in staff time created by reducing the number of processes in the purchasing department.

- Savings in staff time by improving the scheduling of maintenance staff and food service workers.

- Reductions in food waste in the Parent/Child Center by reviewing and changing processes for reporting absences of children.

- Cost savings by instituting energy reduction programs.

- Savings for workman's compensation premiums by reducing accidents in departments through the elimination of safety problems which were identified by staff.

- Time saving and improved college governance by combining the Quality Steering Committee and the Administrative Council into one group which assumed responsibilities for both processes. The Total Quality Leadership Team has become the main policy-making group of the college while assuming responsibility for monitoring the progress of the TQI initiative.[26]

There are also several additional examples of improvement in the instructional areas. These include:

- Improving course scheduling by directly involving faculty. This surprisingly resulted in increased class sizes by an average of more than two students for each class offered.

- Setting maximum class sizes for each offering by the college and establishing productivity ratios calculated by comparing actual class sizes with maximums. This created more equitable course loads and more individualized instruction.

- Determining, through surveys, preferred class times for students and offering classes to accommodate the schedules of working students.

- Improving the efficiency of facilitating small group instruction and using instructional media while providing individualize programs. This enabled students to move from course to course based on the completion of identified competencies. This was accomplished partially by setting up multiple-course laboratories.

- Using TQI tools to establish a world renowned computer integrated manufacturing system which networks the entire campus and integrates computerized student learning systems with business/industrial software and hardware systems.[27]

Do Graduates Leave With TQI Competencies?

The ultimate goal is to graduate students with competencies in the concepts, tools, and techniques of total quality improvement. This requires the faculty to define competencies and integrate them into the instructional programs of the college, and then model them in teaching/learning processes. (Chapter Four described the processes used to integrate TQI competencies into the curriculum.) At Fox Valley, guarantees are issued to both graduates and their employers. With the help of business and industry the college determines measurable quality competencies and organizes a plan to ensure that each graduate has demonstrated competence in each of the quality standards.

This TQI guarantee for graduates certifies that each student will learn the quality standards and use the quality tools effectively. If they do not possess the competencies stated, the college will redo the quality training at no cost.

Has the Culture of the Institution Improved?

Much has been written about changes in the organizational culture as the quality principles of participative management, team problem-solving, customer service, and process management are put into practice. When Fox Valley Technical College implemented TQI in 1985, a survey was initiated to track changes in staff morale and institutional climate.

The Survey of Organizations, published by Rensis Likert Associates, Inc., is an instrument that has 115 items organized into 28 indexes.[28] It was selected by the College because its theoretical base was thought to be compatible with the quality movement. Another reason for its selection was its capability to produce work-unit specific data; that is, satisfaction with supervision, peer relationships, and other aspects of organizational climate broken down by unit. Administrators/managers compared their employees ratings with all other ratings of the College. In all, 34 characteristics were compared.

All college faculty, staff, and administrators are asked to complete the 20-minute survey each year. The response rate averaged over 85%. T-tests were used to identify significant changes in ratings during the first five years. A change of .12 between mean ratings was selected as being an indicator of significant change.

Results showed that when comparing 1992 means to those given in 1987, there were 20 indexes which showed significant increases. Three indexes showed slight decreases over the same period. Carol Mishler, chief researcher for the college, reports that the survey was helpful in identifying areas for improvement in the college as a whole as well as in individual work units. Overall improvement in the survey ratings across six years was found in the following categories:

Communications Flow	*Decision Making*	*Concern for People*
Influence and Control	*Job Challenge*	*Coordination*
Team Building	*Goal Emphasis*	*Work Facilitation*
Participation	*Involvement*	*Supervisor Support*
Supervisor Competence	*Facilitation*	*Administrative Scope*
Goal Emphasis	*Group Work*	*Group Functioning*
Group Integration	*Student Comes First* [29]	

This profound change in organizational culture caused major improvement of services for customers. Throughout the College, faculty and staff identified student needs and put practices in place to meet and exceed them. Examples in improved customer service activities follow:

- Focus Group sessions resulted in student assistance in the design of brochures, establishment of school schedules, conduct of campus tours, and the design of the new student center.

- Work orders in most service departments include a customer evaluation form.

- Programs and services of the college are assessed by external teams using the quality elements.

- There are active advisory groups for each of the 62 programs of the College, representing input from over 700 individuals from outside the campus.

- A customer service committee monitors services, collects survey and suggestion information, and formulates recommended policies for customers.

- Student course evaluations are conducted at least once during each course offering.

Ratings on surveys continue to be very high as employees engage in process improvement activities geared to meeting and exceeding their customer needs.

After several years experience using TQI in an educational setting and following review of the processes used at several other institutions, it can now be confirmed that educational institutions which implement TQI properly can expect to experience, over time, many of the same changes. These changes result in the transformation of the climate and culture of the institution. There will also be changes in the way the faculty and staff organize their work and solve problems.

These benefits will usually occur in small increments in the work units and departments of the College. These lead to system-wide change throughout the institution in the following:

Customer Service	*Staff Relations/Morale*
Problem Solving	*Enrollment Management*
Institutional Planning	*Shared Decision Making*
Attrition Rates	*Community/Business Relations*
Cost Containment	*Accountability and Costing*
Scheduling	*Conduct of Meetings*
Communications	*Image and Public Relations*

SUMMARY COMMENTS

1. The emphasis on the assessment plan should be on prevention rather than inspection.

2. The assessment system should be based on the character and uniqueness of the institution. Comparisons with other institutions should be used primarily for continuous quality improvement.

3. Any successful assessment model requires that the mission statement be carefully written and used as the basis for the design of the system. It should also be reviewed continually.

4. Several different measures should be used to determine progress in an institution.

5. The general approach should be to use both the institutional effectiveness plan and measurements as continuous self-study vehicles which, over time, present a comprehensive picture of how well the institution is fulfilling its mission.

6. The primary priorities of any assessment plan must focus on several bottom-line criteria:

- Is there improved academic achievement by students?

- Have the graduates acquired skills and competencies to make them proficient academically and technically, while correctly using total quality improvement tools and techniques?

- Is there great efficiency and accountability in administration, service, operations, and instruction?

Chapter 7
Success Stories

When Fox Valley Technical College initiated total quality improvement in its instructional programs and services in 1985, there were only a few educational institutions in the Country that were engaged in quality efforts. Most were using quality improvement in service departments or administrative offices. There was little involvement in the instructional programs.

Today, there are a number of institutions throughout the Country and around the world involved on a full-scale basis. Their results have been quite astonishing, however, all agree that there is still a long way to go. Many of these institutions have now surpassed Fox Valley's early effort and are national leaders in the movement. Organizations such as the Continuous Quality Improvement Network (CQIN) continue to promote sharing among the institutions involved. The presidents of those colleges express their commitment to total quality by their willingness to meet regularly and share their experiences. A few have changed the focus of their quality movement and are no longer active promoters of the total quality effort.

This chapter features success stories told by individuals in eleven institutions. They were selected based on their experiences with the USA Group National Quality Academy and they are representative of many other similar success stories. Their willingness to share the challenges and successes they've had enables other educators to learn from their experiences. The stories, told in their own words, describe their efforts in their on-going quest for continuous improvement.

Albuquerque Technical Vocational Institute (TVI)

One of the goals articulated in President Alex Sanchez's inaugural message in October, 1994, was finding management techniques to sharpen the focus on the Albuquerque Technical Vocational Institute's real business—serving students—and increase success with other customers, including employers. Continuous Quality Improvement (CQI) was chosen as the vehicle to make it happen.

In response to the President's CQI goal, a Continuous Quality Improvement Steering Team was established in November, 1994. The team is comprised of students, support staff, faculty, and managers. The team developed its mission, vision, and goal statements and published them in a brochure; developed a CQI plan which has been incorporated into the TVI strategic plan; and wrote a definition of quality for TVI.

The March, 1995 Staff Development Day focused on CQI and included training via interactive TV, broadcast live on the local public-access channel. In June, 1995, staff, faculty, and a student participated in USA Group National Quality Academy's train-the-trainer program. These individuals now serve as a core team of trainers. A quality orientation was developed by some of the trainers using the Plan-Do-Study-Act (PDSA) cycle, and college-wide training began January, 1996.

The Governing Board members and the management team participated in a quality orientation presented by USA Group National Quality Academy also in June, 1995. The Governing Board declared its support for CQI at TVI by unanimously passing the resolution shown in Table 18.

Albuquerque Technical Vocational Institute
Governing Board Resolution 1995–51

Whereas, Continuous Quality Improvement (CQI) is an on-going, organization-wide process for improvement which achieves full customer satisfaction through participation of trained team members using quality measures and techniques; and

Whereas, the state of New Mexico has declared as one of its initiatives the implementation of quality, especially in the education sector; and

Whereas, the mission of the Albuquerque Technical Vocational Institute (TVI) emphasizes quality instruction that enhances employment opportunities and lifelong learning; and

Whereas, qualities such as teamwork, customer focus, process improvement, problem solving, and continuous improvement that prepare students to be successful also need to be valued and practiced by TVI employees; and

Whereas, CQI allows for employee participation at all levels within the organization thereby increasing knowledge and morale; and

Whereas, the needs of the TVI community continually change and meeting these changing needs is essential to the continued success of TVI; and

Whereas, CQI processes provide the tools and knowledge necessary to quickly, efficiently and effectively meet new needs; and

Whereas, an employee steering team representative of all TVI job categories is working to define and plan processes for implementing, maintaining, and operating a continuous quality improvement system at TVI; and

Whereas, CQI will provide more effective and efficient service to all customers; and

Whereas, effective and efficient processes result in cost savings; now, therefore be it

RESOLVED, That the Governing Board of the Albuquerque Technical Vocational Institute declares its support for continuous quality improvement at TVI.

ADOPTED, This 12th day of September, 1995.

Table 18—Albuquerque Technical Vocational Institute
Board Policy on Continuous Quality Improvement

CQI processes spread throughout the Institute during 1995. Quality courses are offered in the Business Occupations, Technologies, and Trades and Service Occupations Departments. Many committees are replacing parliamentary procedure with brainstorming and decision by consensus. Meetings are more productive with vision/mission statements, ground rules, activity diagrams, and feedback. Employee committees have been convened to make recommendations on distance education, budget, parking, faculty pay, the bookstores, and the academic calendar. The CQI process has led to a condensed summer term and, in Trades and Service Occupations, a four-day teaching week.

TVI's flexibility and responsiveness were demonstrated anew with the decision to merge two of its core programs—adult education and developmental studies—to offer more opportunities to students.

Seeking support for improving teaching, counseling, data collection, and decision-making, a successful $1.6 million, five-year grant application was written for TVI's first federal Title III funds.

TVI also focused on how it does business with its sister institutions. Articulation agreements were signed with Albuquerque Public Schools (APS) for concurrent enrollment, with the University of New Mexico (UNM) for engineering and business programs, and with the sheet metal workers for apprenticeships. A joint project with APS developed education transition strategies for mentally disabled students. The Puente Project was formed to introduce fourth-graders to post secondary education and the promise of careers in science. And UNM established a new scholarship for graduates of TVI associate-degree programs who pursue a bachelor's degree.

In the Trades and Service Occupations Department, teams were formed to develop, teach, and continually improve courses. Teams work on ways to improve retention, recruit students, and move from a teaching to a learning delivery system. Employers are included as full partners on teams to help recruit students, eliminate waste, help with retention, share resources, reduce cost, and improve the community. A quality room has been set up for training and meetings. Data collected for student outcomes assessment is being used to make decisions in the

PDSA cycle. Problems and complaints are now viewed as opportunities for improvement. Faculty, staff, and administrators are working in teams as equal partners to define quality, identify customers, examine processes, measure, set goals, and improve. The new culture in the Trades and Service Occupations Department encourages calculated risk taking, aggressive searches for new ideas, and searches for ways to improve. While fear still exists, it is being driven out by looking at systems and processes and not people when problems occur.

The Tutorial/Learning Center (TLC) developed a strategic plan using quality tools. The result of the plan is a better understanding and participation, at all levels, of the TLC's direction, purpose, and goals. A peer recognition program was implemented.

The Business Occupations Department program directors, administrative assistant, and dean are engaged in examining Baldrige criteria and developing an awareness of systems and processes for improvement. The team, with faculty input, is developing a department vision statement and set of core values. They are also planning workshops which focus on CQI in the classroom and the workplace. Other department teams are studying faculty evaluation, student academic achievement, and textbooks.

TVI is participating in the Strengthening Quality in Schools (SQS) initiative. SQS was established by the Governor's Business Executives for Education to provide the expertise needed to develop a world-class quality education system for New Mexico schools. SQS assists in improving a variety of aspects of education using total quality management principles. Several TVI faculty and staff members are assisting Albuquerque Public Schools in assessing current processes and improving those processes.

In a little over a year, CQI has become a common phrase in the Institute's vocabulary. There are increasing numbers of employees who are determining how to do their jobs better. In the spirit of continuous change and improvement, the President's Council now plans to focus on the Malcolm Baldrige Examination Criteria and a realignment team is studying ways in which the instructional departments can break down barriers and eliminate duplication of courses among programs.

Albuquerque TVI
525 Buena Vista SE
Albuquerque, NM 87106

Dr. Alex Sanchez, President

Contact: Ms. Charlotte Martin
Telephone: 505-224-3322

Central Newfoundland Regional College

The Central Newfoundland Regional College (CNRC) of Newfoundland, Canada, adopted a 'Quality First' Policy in April, 1993. In August of the same year, total quality management awareness sessions were held. From the awareness sessions volunteers were recruited to facilitate total quality management training. Since January, 1994, CNRC has been involved in training its personnel. We have concurred that CNRC has transformed to a "learning organization."

Though there have been difficult times, the majority of trained personnel feel quality is what it's all about—providing the best they can for their students and for one another. The training programs have provided us with the tools and techniques to improve our processes and solve problems.

The economic downturn of the province of Newfoundland and the funding impact this has had on all colleges in the province caused us to wonder if quality could be afforded at a time when cost cutting measures were invoked.

In May, 1995 the Adult Basic Education (ABE) program funding was cut from all colleges in Newfoundland. Several Central Newfoundland Regional College ABE instructors were given layoff notices in the midst of doing total quality management training. Morale was down. The Director of Instructional Services sponsored a cross-functional Adult Basic Education team to look at the crisis. Time was at a premium and the team of volunteers, with the help of a facilitator, brainstormed, surveyed, researched, and presented management with some answers regarding how to continue the ABE program. The team performed well.

The Open Learning Delivery Concept for CNRC for Adult Basic Education programming was born. Today, most of the laid-off ABE instructors are employed in contract ABE and Open Learning programs. The remarkable thing about this team is that all members were faculty who had received layoff notices. The bottom line for them was the realization that delivering this much needed program to the community was absolutely necessary. The total quality management concept of "ask the people who do the job" worked as they were able to effectively solve this difficult problem.

The first cross-functional team at the Central Newfoundland Regional College was sponsored by the Director of Finance and Administration to look at the accounts payable process. Team members were selected from five campuses and Headquarters. Once they established their mission statement they were off and running. The new process, recommended by the team, was tested, checked, implemented, and rechecked. Today it is working because it is the process the employees recommended and agreed to implement. The employees know if the process doesn't continue to provide what is needed, the team can go back and apply the Plan-Do-Check-Act (PDCA) cycle once again to reexamine the processes used.

CNRC is still involved in training, still justifying the cost of quality, still focusing on improving communications, and still eroding the skepticism. Imposed economic restraints are not making it easy. What makes the continuous improvement process worthwhile for the believers is hearing "we could solve this with a team"; "the team process worked before"; "now that's not quality"; and the pursuit is definitely worthwhile when you hear "now that is quality."

It is still uncertain whether implementation of total quality management is a complete success at CNRC. The College is facing provincial and federal financial restraints. Restructuring of the College system is being considered and the future of CNRC, as it is today, is unknown. However, for each person touched by the TQM implementation process, Oliver Wendell Holmes said it all in this quote:

"A man's mind stretched by a new idea can never go back to its original dimension."

Central Newfoundland Regional College
Springdale Campus
PO Box 400
Springdale, Newfoundland A0J 1T0
CANADA

Mr. James Forward, President

Contact: Ms. Millie Downey, Quality Coordinator
Telephone: 709-489-5351

Cleary College

Cleary College is a 113 year old, independent, specialized College of Business with campuses in Ypsilanti and Howell, Michigan. Curricula have consistently blended theoretical principles with the application and demonstration of those theories. We believe we have a special responsibility to role model as well as teach effective business principles.

In the Fall of 1989, the College President was challenged by a community business leader to practice quality if we wanted to effectively teach contemporary management and compete in the contracted training arena. In the Winter of 1990, after an assessment of the potential fit with the institution, Cleary College embarked on an organizational transformation.

Our goal was to ensure the long-term health and vitality of the College by economically satisfying our customers through the consistent application of continuous improvement methodology to the alignment and refinement of our academic and administrative systems.

We began with training of the executive staff of the College in Dr. W. Edwards Deming's philosophy of management and specific techniques for customer and system mapping, flow charting, systems work, variation, planned change, and better understanding of people and knowledge. The executive staff at the College had completed one of Dr. Deming's seminars. Faculty and staff also participated in a number of teleconferences, and selected faculty received additional training through a series of external seminars and also assisted external consultants apply these techniques in training contracts with area businesses. This helped build an informed base of knowledge for campus leadership and allowed the College to develop new classroom delivery methodology. Additionally, as process improvement and alignment teams were assembled, team members received specific training in the use of continuous improvement techniques.

The College expanded its training focus and now regularly provides broad-based, college-wide training in customer satisfaction/continuous improvement philosophy and application with all faculty and staff. Currently, six days are dedicated to this training over the course of the academic year, and one afternoon each month is dedicated to conversations on quality among faculty and staff with the College president at each of our two campuses.

In addition to training, one of the first activities the College undertook was the identification of our current and potential customers and the implementation of a concept of *internal* customers. Two primary external customers emerged: the student customer and the business-employer customer. The examination of their needs allowed the College to move to the development of its *core system* map and system purpose definition. This has served to clarify and align efforts at improvement.

The concept of the internal customer resulted in a better appreciation of who relied on whom for information to perform their job, and employee satisfaction appears greater as internal customer needs have been met.

The continual improvement of our systems to provide dependable and economic satisfaction of our customer needs and expectations became our underlying objective. We have continued that process with routine *customer mapping* in which staff and faculty not only talk to their customers, but listen to what is being said so customer needs can be identified and described. With this as a fundamental step in our management system, we are then able to identify measurable criteria that confirm how well the College systems are satisfying those customer needs and expectations. This information provides the basis for system improvement.

This process of system improvement has also been applied to the College's curricular development, review, and refinement, and in fact, forms the basis for the College's *student outcomes assessment* process.

With the perspective of *customer satisfaction* in clear view, we also looked at the various positions at the College and their relationship to customer satisfaction. We realized that our human resources were not properly aligned to deliver consistent product and services. Through this review, we were able to initially reduce the number of full time employees, and to shift remaining resources from the executive, administrative, and support levels to faculty and student advising/service personnel. This process also resulted in a divisional realignment of reporting relationships and a clarification of system responsibilities.

As a result, employees at the College now have a better understanding of how the systems they own operate as subsystems of the College's core systems, and are learning how to implement formal systems alignment processes (following the steps of the Shewhart Cycle) to drive even greater customer satisfaction.

In this alignment process, care is given to follow Dr. Deming's advice to attempt a "logical basis for allocation of responsibilities" so that "everyone involved... know in advance what he will be accountable for."

This organizational realignment has significantly and positively improved each divisional area of the College. Each division is now better able to focus on its own *core systems*, and a better sense of system relationships has emerged. Our academic division, for example, now focuses primarily on the teaching-learning system and its various support systems. (Previously this division also had responsibility for various student service subsystems and enrollment sales). Our finance division now focuses on the systems required to achieve financial equilibrium and the *manageability* of financial subsystems by nonfinancial managers. (Previously, some major financial subsystems reported elsewhere). Finally, our college relations division is able to focus on the internal and external *community and people relations* systems necessary to generate revenue through advancement and enrollment management. (Previously, these systems were in separate divisions and resulted in duplication of effort and communication gaps). This organizational system alignment has introduced the type of organizational structure that Stephen Covey proposes in which the subsystems are aligned in the same direction...the resultant synergy and dynamism is incredible.

During the period of initial review of the College organization, we simultaneously instituted the careful control of expenditures in areas that were less critical to the satisfaction of customer needs and expectation, thus slowing the percentage of increase of expenditures against revenue. This not only modestly reduced expenses, but also allowed the reallocation of dollars to areas of greater impact on customer satisfaction.

The College then moved to a short term analysis of academic products to identify major weaknesses and opportunities to better satisfy current and potential student customers. This led to the elimination of several academic programs that were no longer meeting customer needs nor affording our graduates a competitive position as they sought entry or movement within the job market. It also confirmed that the curricular mix at the College under served the *nontraditional*, adult market that the College thought it had been serving well. We also learned that our curriculum was inadequate to meet the needs that our business/employer customers projected for their current and future work force. This led to the implementation of a new competency based curriculum, strengthened business advisory partnerships, and new curricular offerings.

Initially, new programs were targeted at the under served adult market and offered in a weekend format, which resulted in substantial enrollment growth. Subsequent improvements to the College's systems of transfer and alternative credit (portfolio, tests, etc.) have resulted in even more *customer-friendly* systems and increased satisfaction. Not surprisingly, our focus on customer satisfaction resulted in a five percent improvement in retention rates.

The application of this new knowledge and skill that faculty and staff have acquired has also enabled the College to begin specific academic programs and courses in the theory and application of continuous improvement and quality management. Our classroom focus and our management and philosophical beliefs have become more closely aligned. This new knowledge and skill have also allowed the College to develop a highly effective contracted training program and become a direct and effective contributor to local businesses in leading them through their own transformations toward continuously improving customer satisfaction.

Another natural outgrowth of the new understandings of mission and purpose that our customer satisfaction focus has brought has been a dramatic change in our approach to institutional planning, both long and short range. We now have a planning system that ensures this important function receives attention during the year through quarterly day-long "planning retreats" of the executive staff. This system is structured to offer a traditional Strengths-Weaknesses-Opportunities-Threats (SWOT) analysis.

Our planning model requires participation by staff and faculty in the shaping of decisions, the examination of data for planned change and adjustments, the collaborative development of the broader vision of the college, agreement on the short term goals, and cooperation on cross divisional system alignment to achieve both the short term goals and the long term vision.

The demonstrable impact of satisfying customer needs and applying continuous improvement methodology was better control of expenses and a 51% increase in tuition revenue. These actions allowed the elimination of $428,000 accrued operating deficit over a three year period; an increase in the number of faculty and staff (13%); replacement of student computer resources (100% upgrade); and improved student to computer ratios (9 to 1 from 20 to 1).

Externally, the image of the college improved to the point where we were sought out to provide leadership for local county-wide quality initiatives, praised by the local press for our mission focus, and recognized nationally (an eleventh national ranking among business schools by *US News & World Report*). We were also able to issue a tax-exempt bond, in which the agent placed the entire issue in forty eight hours, causing the observation that "the College has an excellent reputation." We believe there is also a relationship between our institutional transformation progress and Dr. W. Edwards Deming having agreed to accept an honorary degree from the College in June, 1994.

Most importantly, however, our efforts at "customer mapping," the economic satisfaction of customer needs, the application of systems theory and planned change theory, and the understanding of variation, have changed the very fabric of the College. Our employees, as well as our student and business/employer customers, have more knowledge and greater problem solving skills. We approach problems differently and look for common and special cause in our systems variation. Our people are more comfortable in exercising their authority and ability to improve our systems to better satisfy our customers. As Dr. Deming encourages, we strive for "joy in work."

Cleary College
2170 Washtenaw Avenue
Ypsilanti, Michigan 48197

Dr. Thomas Sullivan, President

**Contact: Mr. Vince Linder, Vice President of Academic Affairs
Telephone: 313-483-4400**

Guilford Technical
Community College

In August, 1992, Guilford Technical Community College (GTCC) managers were introduced to continuous quality improvement principles in a workshop conducted by trainers from Gilbarco, Inc., a major international manufacturing company in Greensboro. At the close of the two and a half day session, President Don Cameron and the managers made a commitment to begin the quality journey with a destination focused on improving the educational programs and services provided to GTCC students. The president was particularly interested in targeting quality efforts in the classroom, with an emphasis on improving the teaching and learning processes.

In January, 1993, the GTCC Building Quality Together (BQT) initiative was introduced on campus. From January through June following that announcement, all 425 full-time employees participated in eight hours of "Continuous Improvement Awareness" training focused on the major concepts of leadership, customer focus, teamwork, and PDCA methodology. At the end of that awareness training, employees identified three program strands for additional development and training: (1) teamwork; (2) process improvement; and (3) quality applications in the classroom. In addition, twenty-eight employees volunteered to actively participate in the design and delivery of programs to meet these identified needs.

During the second year, 1993-94, of GTCC's quality initiative, all managers participated in twelve hours of teamwork training and three project teams were given training in process improvement. Some of the major outcomes of teamwork training were measurable improvement in the effectiveness and efficiency of staff and committee meetings and increased satisfaction ratings from meeting participants.

The most exciting quality program strand was the development of a faculty training program focused on applying quality concepts to improve the teaching and learning processes in the classroom. A twelve member faculty team worked collaboratively to design the CLASS (Continuous Learning Assures Student Success) program during the 1993-94 year. This innovative program has three major instructional modules: (1) The Quality Classroom; (2) The Teacher/Learner Team; and (3) Teaching/Learning Process Improvement. (An outline of the program modules and learning outcomes is shown as Table 19.)

FACULTY DEVELOPMENT
Program - At - A - Glance

Title: **CLASS: Continuous Learning Assures Student Success**

CQC Member:	Guilford Technical Community College P.O. Box 309, Jamestown, NC 27282	Contact: Diane Gibson (910) 334-4822, Ext. 2550
Program Length:	Overview: 1 hour, Seminar: 12 hours, Maximum Number of Participants: 25	Train-The-Trainer: 2 days

Program Description: The quality of teaching and learning in community college classrooms is essential to the future success of these institutions. The purpose of the CLASS program, designed by faculty for faculty, is to apply CQI principles and explore a variety of strategies in the classroom to continuously improve the quality of these critical processes.

Major Modules and Topics:

Module 1:   The Quality Classroom (3hrs.)
- Introduction to the Class Model
- Classroom CQI Assumptions
- Characteristics of A Quality Classroom
- 14 Obligations of Instructors

Module 2:   The Teacher/Learner Team (4.5hrs.)
- Capacity in Student Diversity
- Instructor/Student Needs, Expectations, and Boundaries
- Classroom Team Building and Cooperative Learning
- Introduction to the Theory of Multiple Intelligences

Module 3: Teaching/Learning Process Improvement (4.5hrs.)
- Five Types of Teaching Strategies
- Continuous Improvement of Instructional Design
- Content Application
- Classroom Research and Assessment Techniques

Learning Outcomes: At the close of the training, participants will be able to:

1. Discuss and categorize the characteristics associated with a quality classroom.
2. Relate continuous improvement assumptions to the classroom environment.
3. Apply Deming's 14 Obligations of Management to Instructors.
4. Define the diversity which exists in community college classrooms and recognize the learning capacity in that diversity.
5. Recognize and appreciate the needs and expectations of the Teacher/Learner Team.
6. Incorporate the five basic elements of cooperative learning into a classroom activity.
7. Discuss the Theory of Multiple Intelligences and assess MI of their students.
8. Define five types of teaching strategies and the strengths and weaknesses of each type.
9. Incorporate knowledge of content, teaching strategies, and student learning styles in instructional plans.
10. State the purpose of classroom research and use a minimum of five classroom assessment strategies.

Instructors: All sessions are conducted by faculty and staff members who have applied these strategies in their classrooms.

Target Audience: Full and part-time faculty members and instructional administrators.

Table 19—CLASS: Continuous Learning Assures Student Success

The CLASS program was piloted in June, 1994, and revised based on faculty input before implementing it campus-wide during the 1994-95 year. The program was designed for faculty to attend four three-hour sessions, one each week. In between sessions, faculty are expected to complete identified strategies or activities in their classrooms and come prepared with the results to the next session.

The GTCC quality initiative experienced significant growth during 1994-95, both on campus and in the state. In July, 1994, GTCC became the host college for the Carolina Quality Consortium, a collaborative community college network, funded by the North Carolina Community College System for a three year period. The mission of the consortium is to communicate continuous quality improvement concepts and strengthen practices in the North Carolina Community College System and member colleges. To date 21 of the 58 colleges in the state with active quality initiatives have joined the consortium.

Internally, the BQT initiative focused on process improvement opportunities and CLASS program implementation. All employees participated in "Process Improvement: Teams and Tools" training, an eight-hour program designed to provide staff with a general awareness of the steps that a project team would complete and the tools which could be used in the study of an improvement project. An additional 12 project teams began their studies during the 1994-95 year and three teams completed the projects which began the previous year. In October, 1995, GTCC received two David Pierce Quality Awards from the National Initiative for Leadership and Institutional Effectiveness at the Team Building for Quality Conference. The first award was presented to President Don Cameron for Organizational Leadership and the second was a Quality Team award presented to a project team for their outstanding work in improving the travel approval process.

The CLASS program remained a major focus during 1994-95. It was conducted with GTCC faculty as well as faculty from other community Colleges in North Carolina through the Carolina Quality Consortium. Currently, over 200 faculty have completed the training and it is anticipated that an additional 150 faculty will complete the program by June, 1996. Feedback from faculty participants over the past two years has been extremely positive and suggestions for improvement have been incorporated into the current program. The CLASS program will be expanded during 1996 to provide more in-depth training in the design and application of cooperative learning, learning styles research, and assessment techniques to improve the quality of teaching and learning in community college classrooms.

Guilford Technical Community College is in the fourth year of its quality journey. Management has just completed a self-assessment on three of the seven Malcolm Baldrige Award categories. The assessment revealed that we have successfully moved from a fire fighting organization to an emerging organization that recognizes the need to continually focus on meeting, or exceeding, the changing needs of our students for quality educational programs and services.

Guilford Technical Community College
Main Campus
PO Box 309
Jamestown, NC 27282

Dr. Donald Cameron, President

Contact: Dr. Diane Gibson
Telephone: 910-334-4822 Ext. 2550

Illinois Eastern
Community Colleges

In the Fall of 1994, shortly after Dr. Ron Hutkin assumed the position of Chancellor at Illinois Eastern Community Colleges, a multi-college district in southeastern Illinois, it was obvious to everyone that immediate change was needed. Faculty and staff morale was at an all-time low, colleges constantly bickered between themselves about trivial matters, any sense of district identity was totally absent, and many faculty and staff were preparing to leave before the proverbial *ship* went down.

Dr. Hutkin immediately asked the Dean of Inter-Campus Affairs, Jack Davis, to coordinate a TQM orientation session for a cross-section of IECC faculty, staff, and students. A special session was to be scheduled for the IECC Board of Trustees. Davis contacted Dr. Stanley Spanbauer of USA Group National Quality Academy in Appleton, Wisconsin, and arranged for Dr. Spanbauer and Jo Hillman to come to IECC and present a program on how the principals of TQM could be applied to a community college environment.

Dr. Spanbauer and Jo Hillman visited IECC for two days in early December, 1994, and presented three TQM orientation workshops—one for faculty and staff, one for senior administration, and one for the Board of Trustees. The evaluations of the three workshops were overwhelmingly positive. It was apparent to all who read the evaluations that faculty, staff, students, administration, and Board of Trustees felt that a major organizational management paradigm shift from a hierarchi-cal-oriented organizational structure to a TQM-based management was most de-sirable.

IECC devised a four-phase TQM initiative whereby the IECC Board of Trustees approved $108,000 of TQM related expenditures over a two-year period. Phase One involved providing all 354 full-time employees with at least forty-five contact hours of TQM professional development most relevant to their assigned responsi-bilities. The training was to begin on July 1, 1995, and completed by June 30, 1996. Participation was to be voluntary.

IECC arranged for Dr. Spanbauer and Jo Hillman to come to Olney, Illinois in April of 1995, to present a week-long Train-the-Trainer workshop at IECC for 40 selected faculty, staff, and students. This trained core would then become TQM workshop facilitators for other IECC faculty, staff, and students. *Quality Process Training for Service and Support Personnel* was offered to all secretarial, custo-dial, maintenance, and technical staffs. *Continuous Improvement Strategies in Education* was offered to all administrative (Chancellor, presidents, deans, etc.) and other middle and upper management staff. *Quality Training for Instructors* was offered to all full-time faculty.

Phase Two involved implementing new Associate of Applied Science (AAS) de-gree and certificate programs in both Total Quality Management and Industrial Quality Management. It was determined that purchasing a ten-course (30 semes-ter hours) curriculum from USA Group National Quality Academy would enable IECC to begin offering the courses in these programs much earlier than if the curriculum were developed in-house. The AAS and one-year certificate programs in Total Quality Management were the first TQM programs approved by the Illi-nois Community Colleges Board (April 1995) and the Illinois Board of Higher Education (July 1995) in the State of Illinois.

Phase Three involved becoming established as a Regional Quality Academy. As a Regional Quality Academy, affiliated with USA Group National Quality Academy, we felt that we could offer the same TQM professional development workshops that we had received to others in a larger area. On April 18, 1995, in ceremonies in

Olney, Illinois, IECC became the first Regional Quality Academy. The IECC Regional Quality Academy has exclusive license to market various National Quality Academy and Noel-Levitz workshops and printed materials in the states of Illinois, Indiana, and Missouri. Mr. Harry L. Crisp, Chairman of the Illinois Community College Board, said at the presentation that "The IECC involvement in total quality management is an outstanding initiative. Thank you (IECC) for the great job you're doing for the people of Illinois." Illinois Governor Jim Edgar, visited IECC in June of 1995, and stated "IECC's new TQM initiative is a 'model' that other community colleges will undoubtedly want to follow."

Phase Four involved establishing a regional TQM resource center with printed, audio visual, and other training materials available for loan throughout the IECC district as well as the license area of the IECC Regional Quality Academy. Although we have already acquired many resource materials, we will continue to work with local business and industry to house materials beneficial to their needs.

This Phase also included the formation of the Illinois Eastern Community Colleges Total Quality Leadership Team. The TQL Team is charged with recommended processes:

1. To improve communication and the flow of information.

2. To serve as a forum for student and employee quality-related issues.

3. To improve the strategic planning, budgeting, and student assessment.

4. To improve curricula and programs.

5. To produce a return on the investment of the taxpayers in the district.

The initial TQL Team membership was selected by a committee comprised of representatives from all employee groups to ensure that all employee groups and all four colleges and the district office have representation on the TQL Team. At present, the TQL Team is completing their operational guidelines. It is planned that the team will become operational in March of 1996.

After all of this TQM professional development training one should logically ask, "Have things really changed?" I submit that if you were to visit with faculty and staff at IECC today, I'm sure they would emphatically tell you that the change has been remarkable. Faculty and staff at the Colleges now converse with their colleagues at sister colleges. Staff are no longer afraid to ask questions or state their opinions. Faculty and staff morale is at an all-time high and many employees have said that they have stopped looking for employment outside of IECC. Truly, the tide has changed.

However, what we've accomplished thus far has not been easy. Many IECC faculty, middle managers, and administrators are still reluctant to embrace any philosophical change they do not fully understand, especially one whereby they might potentially be forced to empower their subordinates. Tactically, we've decided to adopt a *go slow* policy on TQM changes to ensure that our implementation will be more successful in the long term.

On a more positive note, some of our administration and middle managers totally support the paradigm shift. Classified staff (secretaries, custodians) and professional staff are the most supportive of the district's TQM initiative. After all, they are the ones who are being empowered. Almost all staff, whether or not they totally support the management style change, appreciate the opportunity to have participated in a total quality management professional development workshop activity.

The next step in the IECC implementation process is to form a TQM Planning Committee to recommend a Quality First Plan that will guide the implementation of TQM throughout the college district. When the Quality First Plan is approved by the Board of Trustees, team forming and training will begin at the Colleges and at the district office.

The IECC Board of Trustees, Dr. Hutkin, and the IECC administration are dedicated to and strongly support the organizational management changes being brought about by the TQM implementation process. Although we all know that the IECC TQM implementation process is a journey of several years, we're happy to have begun the journey.

Illinois Eastern Community Colleges
233 East Chestnut Street
Olney, Illinois 62450-2298

Dr. Ron Hutkin, Chancellor

**Contact: Mr. Jackie L. Davis, Dean of Continuous Improvement and Customer Services
Telephone: (618) 393-2982
Fax: (618) 392-4816**

Lamar Community College

Lamar Community College (LCC) is now in the sixth year of its implementation of Total Quality Management (TQM). Gone are the slogans and the vocabulary, but what remains is a solid team-based and customer-oriented structure. The complex nature of the institution has been recognized and organizational evolution is in progress.

Six years ago, Lamar Community College began to build a better way. The management team concept was implemented in Instruction and Student Services. Instructional management teams were born out of necessity: the Vocational Dean and Vice President of Instruction had resigned. Management teams took hold, and remained a strong part of the organization after the current Dean and Vice President were hired. The influences were immediate. The school calendar and course schedule became faculty-supervised processes. The management teams serve as core groups for search and screen hiring processes. In recent years, Business Services has formed a management team.

The North Central Association accreditation process gave Lamar Community College further opportunities for Quality Improvement. In the second year of the implementation of TQM, the North Central Association's Self-Study was conducted, using the management teams as information-gathering bodies. Three years later, interdisciplinary teams were used to answer North Central's concerns with enrollment management, total quality management, and information management at LCC.

Other examples of interdisciplinary, cross-functional teams are the Lamar Community College Learning Resources Center Advisory Committee and the Bookstore Advisory Committee. These committees provide campus-wide input into areas in which many LCC employees are stakeholders. Another area of cross-functional activity is the Access Team, which focuses on eliminating barriers to student enrollment.

Early in the Quality process the need for coordinating teams was identified. FACT (Facilitators And [Division] Chairs Team) was formed, as the name implies, from instructional management team facilitators and division chairs from all instructional disciplines. FACT became the body which addressed interdisciplinary learning issues and developed instructional positions on campus-wide issues. FACT has become an integral part of the Lamar Community College organization. Following the success of FACT, the Student Services Coordinating Team was implemented as FACT's counterpart in Student Services.

Most recently, two top-level teams were formed. The All Campus Management Team, consisting of representatives from all areas of the campus, handles campus-wide issues such as budgeting and strategic planning. The other team is the Executive Leadership Team. The ELT is composed of the President and the Vice President, and provides the top-level sign off and support needed for some activities either by their nature (e.g. very large expenditures) or by external requirements.

The organizational structure that has emerged at Lamar Community College is shown in Table 20.

ALL CAMPUS MANAGEMENT TEAM RELATIONSHIPS

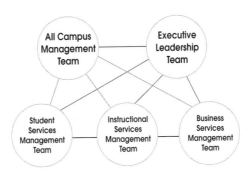

Table 20—Lamar Community College Organizational Structure

Issues can emerge at any level: They can then move up, down, or sideways to be examined thoroughly and dealt with effectively.

Recently, another role emerged for the All Campus Management Team (ACMT). ACMT now also functions as the "Coordinating Teams coordinating team" to develop positions on issues which reflect the broadest possible input.

LCC has an organizational structure that is team-based from top to bottom and also has the organization coupling needed to improve information flow throughout the organization. No structure is perfect, but effective organizations evolve. This is LCC's current state of organizational growth: the future may hold some surprises that this organization would have to adapt to, but those adaptations will be built on this structure, not on a traditional vertical Table of Organization.

Lamar Community College
2401 South Main
Lamar, Colorado 81052

Dr. Marvin Lane, President

Contact: Mr. Richard Lovell
Telephone: 719-336-2248

North Dakota
State College of Science

Recognizing that a good reputation does not guarantee continued success, NDSCS began a journey toward continuous quality improvement in June, 1991. The college has demonstrated its serious commitment to this process through continuous growth and support. The momentum continues with a halftime quality coordinator and eight trainers who teach formal classes on the NDSCS campus and to the states served by the Northland Regional Quality Academy—Minnesota, northern part of South Dakota, Wyoming, North Dakota, Montana. A Quality Council, established with representation from all employee groups, guides the process on the NDSCS campus.

As applied on our campus, Total Quality is an analytical thinking process as well as a commitment of resources to action. Through strategic action plans, developed on an annual basis, strategic-driven goal concepts are addressed and actions taken following a Plan-Do-Check-Act (PDCA) cycle.

Historically, administrative and instructional decisions have been made almost exclusively on personal and professional opinions. Past experience dominated the decision-making process rather than using present needs or future judgment projections to drive decisions. Quality training, commitment, staff empowerment, and quality tools are changing the process. As a result of the quality movement, we have a wealth of data and are building relationships to improve the quality of the decisions. Table 21 identifies faculty, staff, and administrative employees who have participated in training workshops on the NDSCS campus since the inception of Total Quality Training in 1992.

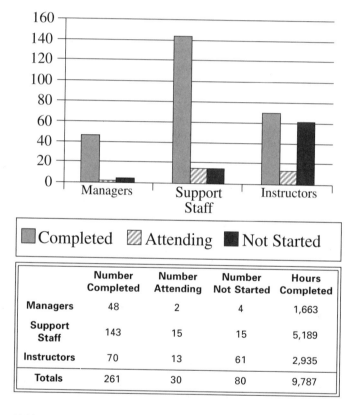

NDSCS
TOTAL QUALITY TRAINING
Number Attending by Group
November 1995

	Number Completed	Number Attending	Number Not Started	Hours Completed
Managers	48	2	4	1,663
Support Staff	143	15	15	5,189
Instructors	70	13	61	2,935
Totals	261	30	80	9,787

Table 21—NDSCS Personnel Who Participated in Quality Training

The pace of change is one of the critical issues facing the College today. Amidst the numerous complexities of their roles and responsibilities, college leadership is trying to successfully manage and capitalize on Total Quality concepts in an effective manner. As we adapt to change we ask these questions: can the change stand the test of time, does the change make a significant impact on the College, will the change place us in a position to serve our students and business/industry needs?

We control our own destiny rather than being controlled by change, through continuous reexamination of organizational structure, the nurturing of a positive campus culture, and measuring the acceptance of the quality movement.

One component of our current strategy is to conduct employee surveys to determine how well NDSCS is growing and learning. The results of the surveys help NDSCS keep, obtain, or balance key operational elements; namely—core capabilities; guiding visions; performance standards; prototype testing/learning; ownership/commitment and integration of people and vision within the initiative of Total Quality.

Through the surveys, we know:

- What students and employees think about the direction in which we are headed.

- What avenues need to be emphasized to reach our employees, our students, and our goals.

- What margins we have and what capabilities need to be developed for NDSCS to remain competitive and to fulfill its purposes.

FALL 1995 EMPLOYEE SURVEY RESULTS

The results of the 1995 Faculty & Staff Survey have been compiled and compared to the 1993 and 1994 surveys. The comparison of the data shows that employees (with 68% of faculty and staff responding) answered most (18 of 23) questions on the survey in a more positive manner in 1995. The answers to the questions that NDSCS employees responded to most positively in 1993, 1994, and 1995 are reported in Table 22.

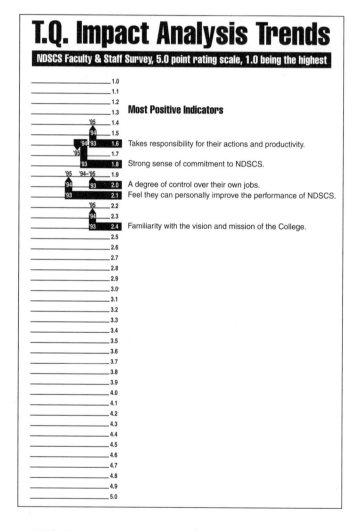

T.Q. Impact Analysis Trends

NDSCS Faculty & Staff Survey, 5.0 point rating scale, 1.0 being the highest

Most Positive Indicators

1.6 — Takes responsibility for their actions and productivity.

1.8 — Strong sense of commitment to NDSCS.

2.0 — A degree of control over their own jobs.
2.1 — Feel they can personally improve the performance of NDSCS.

2.4 — Familiarity with the vision and mission of the College.

Table 22—Most Positive Indicators of Change Identified by NDSCS Employees in Surveys Conducted in 1993-94-95

It was also decided to determine the total quality impact trends regarding the areas of greatest change in the institution. Over the three-year period, the four areas showing the greatest amount of change are illustrated in Table 23. Note that three of them involve changes related to human resources. The fourth area shows the decline in the number of skeptics who present obstacles to the quality improvement effort.

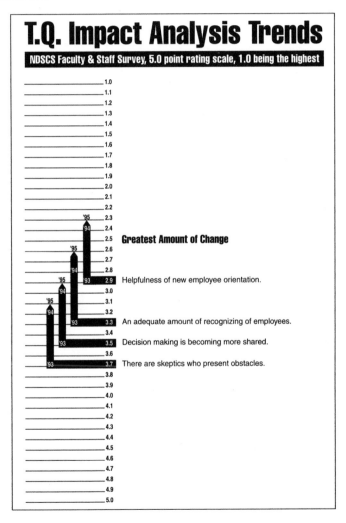

Table 23—Areas Showing Greatest Amount of Positive Change at NDSCS

Employees were also asked to identify the areas most in need of improvement. Those areas which appeared most often during the three years of the survey were as follows:

- Dissemination of Information to Employees

- Levels of Authority

- Shared Decision Making

- Obstacles to Change Created by Skeptics

SUMMARY

As the administration and the Quality Council reviewed the wealth of information gathered through the annual surveys, they decided that the institution should focus on five quality improvement factors to keep the trends moving in a positive direction. A summary of those factors follows:

1. Continue Quality Training

Continuous education/training will assist in improving communication and reducing skepticism while developing a greater familiarity with the Vision and Mission of the College. This is being implemented through a wide range of professional development activities, coupled with supervisory reinforcement of the concepts by keeping staff informed. All this will be monitored by continuing to analyze employee survey results to determine changes in morale and attitudes.

2. Expand Team Culture

The transformation of the culture of NDSCS will continue to be apparent as greater input is provided by a wide range of personnel. As employees participate in problem solving on departmental and cross-functional teams, they will feel more empowered and will feel more committed to the campus movement. Supervisory staff should be encouraged to monitor teams as they progress in decision-making activities.

3. Flatten Organizational Structure

At NDSCS, the organization has been streamlined structurally and numerically. This will not necessarily reduce the levels and layers of decision making until employees see that shared decisions and ownership result. Those who feel motivated and inspired will use mistakes as learning tools. The identification of performance levels expected from each employee will lead to solutions to problems having total campus impact. This can be managed best by employees closest to the action.

4. Strengthen Performance Appraisal Process

Performance appraisal should not be seen as a threat, but as an indication of formative, developmental, and continuous improvement for each employee. NDSCS performances should be based upon current and accurate job descriptions, action plans and/or goals, general criteria, and customer/subordinate/student feedback. Traditional evaluation methods that are typically summarative in nature (evaluation after the fact) have not been effective in reaching the overall goal of professional and personal employee growth. The primary purpose of performance appraisal should be to improve the effectiveness of employees in their various areas of responsibility. Since the success of NDSCS hinges upon each and every individual at the College, it is the employees that distinguish a truly great institution from an average one.

5. Develop Acceptance Through Communication

For all employees to feel they are part owner of the campus, communication must flow across all personnel levels. Employees have accepted the Vision and Mission of the campus and are part of the effort to instill the direction to those on and off the campus.

By being involved, employee actions will make a difference. Action Plans from individual employees will address problem areas on the campus.

Open communication is essential in every unit of the College. Representation from every employee group and students on the Campus Council is needed to specifically implement a process to identify problems, seek alternative solutions, report the action, and continuously measure progress that is observable to all.

We recognize that we must do more than remediate symptoms and perceptions as reported in surveys. We stand ready to go beyond the symptoms, to deal with fundamental issues, and to invoke our own higher thinking skills to discover new concepts to form a frame of reference to internalize quality and make lasting improvement at NDSCS.

North Dakota State College of Science
800 Sixth Street North
Wahpeton, ND 58076-0002

Dr. Jerry Olson, President

Contact: Ms. Gloria Dohman, Quality Coordinator
Telephone: 701-671-2619

Palau Community College

In 1995, Palau Community College (PCC) made a decision that would ultimately alter the community's perception of the College, including PCC personnel themselves. The decision was quite a simple one: PCC would invest a substantial amount of its financial resources on its human resources. The rest, as people say, is history.

A year before, the College had sent three staff to Appleton, Wisconsin to explore the concepts and principles behind the Total Quality Improvement (TQI) movement. This resulted in the College's decision to embark on a journey to become a leader in quality service in the whole Republic of Palau. The journey began in January, 1995, with PCC contracting Dr. Stanley Spanbauer, President and Ms. Jo Hillman, Vice President of USA Group National Quality Academy in Appleton, to deliver training and expose the College to TQI.

During that training, sixteen selected PCC staff underwent Train-The-Trainer workshops and have since conducted the *Quality Process Training for Service and Support Personnel* training program for appropriate PCC employees. Subsequent training on *TQM (Total Quality Management) in the Classroom* and *Continuous Improvement Strategies in Education* will be delivered as well.

Palau Community College opted to implement TQI on its campus to meet two purposes:

1. Establish a continuous improvement process at PCC within which there is always ongoing improvement of the quality of services the College provides its customers; and,

2. Provide PCC staff an opportunity to learn new skills and techniques in servicing customers with quality service.

As of December, 1995, sixty-two of the one hundred and thirty-three PCC employees have attended the *Quality Process Training for Service and Support Personnel* program. All sixty-two individuals have expressed nothing but positive comments on the program's content, presentation, and its facilitators. One particular employee who has worked at the College for over twenty-one years, having finished the training, thanked PCC for bringing back to the forefront the values and principles he always believed but seemed to forget over the years.

Another indication of TQI at work in PCC is last year's Thanksgiving lunch at the College cafeteria. On an initiative of their own, the TQI champs, as we call those who have finished the training, organized themselves and decorated the cafeteria and even helped prepare and serve lunch! This is something PCC has not seen before and everyone was very excited about that. Furthermore, on Tuesday, February 20, 1996, the entire Palau Community College community devoted the whole day at a workshop entitled *Sharing Dreams*. The workshop's objective was to gather input from individual employees as to where PCC will be in the year 2007. Putting the affinity process, brainstorming, and grounding circles to work ensured everyone's participation. The comment from one faculty member was, "We should do this type of activity more often. It gives us an opportunity to be heard as well as feel that our ideas are important to the College."

While these examples may seem trivial in nature, one cannot but help remember that phrase learned in the training which goes something like, "Quality is doing a thousand tiny little things a little bit better".

A most recent development in the College's TQI movement is its decision to become a Regional Quality Academy in association with USA Group National Quality Academy. On January 15, 1996, Mr. Francis M. Matsutaro, PCC President and Dr. Spanbauer signed a contract establishing PCC as the *Pacific Rim Regional Quality Academy*. This historic occasion was witnessed by the College community, the Honorable Tommy E. Remengesau, Jr., Vice President of the Republic of Palau, and representatives of the Palau business industry.

This strategic move not only affiliates PCC with USA Group, Noel-Levitz, and the National Quality Academy, but also enables PCC to spread the concept and applications of TQI throughout Palau and the region (Micronesia and the Philippines) so that more people may benefit. Furthermore, PCC now has the full array of programs to offer in its TQI training arsenal!

This direction PCC has chosen is evidence to anyone that the College truly believes it can *make a difference*, and is committed to serve its customers and community by providing the best quality service it possibly can. Granted, it is understandable for us to experience moments of apprehension and uncertainty at this point in the journey; however, one takes heart in the fact that Palau Community College has seen firsthand what TQI has done for Fox Valley Technical College. This helps PCC focus on its vision of becoming the premier institution in the region in the not too distant future!

Palau Community College
Koror, Republic of Palau 96940

Mr. Francis M. Matsutaro, President

Contact: Ms. Wilma Sukrad, Managing Director
Telephone: (680) 488-2470 or 2471

Rio Salado Community College

When Rio Salado Community College in Phoenix, Arizona began its quality journey in 1991, the faculty and staff were looking for ways to operate more efficiently, improve communication, and broaden employee involvement in governance. A nontraditional college, Rio Salado has seven administrative sites, serves 24,000 students annually, employs 500 adjunct faculty, utilizes 250 classroom sites, and provides educational services across 9,226 square miles of Maricopa County in Arizona. Total Quality Management (TQM) offered a philosophy and methodology for helping to manage such a challenging institution.

With support and encouragement from the college president for an aggressive approach to planning and problem solving, Rio Salado began to shift from the old ways through the continual use of cross-functional, vertically integrated teams utilizing quality skills and techniques. The College vision statement was created and the mission statement was revised and both continue to serve as guiding beacons for the future. Staff and faculty were encouraged to envision *new* approaches, not dwell on old remedies. Coupled with a realistic understanding of financial constraints, enthusiastic staff and faculty created an action plan which incorporated continual change as its only constancy. Other staff and faculty developed the following documents:

- Principles of Quality Learning
- Guidelines and Expectations for Quality Faculty
- Guidelines and Expectations for a Quality College

Many initial results of the quality effort were tangible and definable. These included reducing the cost of producing the College schedule by 13% and reducing rework by 28%; improving the student drop/add process and reducing $15,000 in bad debts; and developing new degree programs in less than half the time previously required. Over time, improvements in student completion rates have been demonstrated as noted in Table 24.

Certificates and Degree Completion

	1986–87	87–88	88–89	89–90	90–91	91–92	92–93	93–94	94–95
Total Certificates	112	171	295	395	250	208	282	207	410
Total Degrees	123	106	128	89	79	94	108	175	141

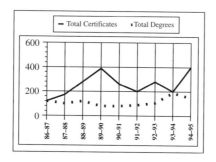

Table 24—Rio Salado Degree and Certificate Completion Rates (1986–95)

Two years into the effort, Rio Salado won the 1993 Arizona Governor's Pioneer Award for Quality, a mini Malcolm Baldrige competition, and, in 1994, Rio Salado participated in the United States Department of Commerce National Institute of Standards and Technology Education Pilot Evaluation process. This professional review stated clearly the impact of the first three years of Rio Salado's quality effort:

- College's focus on internal and external customers' needs is clear.

- Evidence of systemic approaches and early deployment is obvious.

- High satisfaction rate and increasing completion rates of students are evident.

- President and executive leadership efforts are visible and consistent.

- Rio Salado's strengthened approach to curriculum and educational design is evident.

In keeping with the need for decisions based on fact and data, Rio Salado regularly conducted employee surveys to measure trends and movement. While a positive review by the Department of Commerce is noteworthy, measurement of trends in employee knowledge and attitudes is more indicative of the cultural and process impact of the Rio Salado quality journey.

In four years, Rio Salado employees moved from 60 percent knowledge and personal understanding of the college mission to 91 percent. The extent to which employees feel involved in administrative decisions affecting their jobs increased from 56–82 percent. Employee belief that they received administrative support in the performance of their jobs rose from 74–84 percent and various composite rankings regarding rewards and recognition and communications increased from 68–76 percent. Other rankings involving teamwork and flow of information increased somewhat during this same period, as did the faculty and employees' perceived satisfaction of student needs and expectations.

As a result of the quality initiative at Rio Salado, the educational paradigms operating in 1991 have been challenged and processes improved. Customer satisfaction, employee involvement in decision making, and the institutional culture have been broadened and enhanced. More importantly, as a result of the quality efforts, Rio Salado has been transformed from a community college utilizing Total Quality Management techniques and tools to a college facing the future as a truly committed learning organization. Lifelong learning, continuous improvement, and customer focus have replaced the previous institutional culture.

When Rio Salado began its quality journey, it was assumed that change would occur. But, in a relatively short period of time—four years—change has been broader, deeper, and more lasting than anyone first imagined. The quality movement in education was the catalytic converter to move Rio Salado from a nontraditional college probing new methods of education and delivery to a college of the future committed to continuous learning and constantly testing the limits of tradition.

Rio Salado Community College

2323 W. 14th Street

Tempe, Arizona 85281

Dr. Linda Thor, President

Contact: Sharon Koberna
Telephone: 602-223-4000

Shelton State Community College

Shelton State has based its mission in the context of *quality* since its inception and those efforts have positioned the institution as the largest two-year college in the Alabama College System. Not until its connection with USA Group National Quality Academy, however, did College personnel have some structure and tools to help them in a systematic *quest for quality*.

After years of being housed in a strip mall and seriously outdated facilities, Shelton is currently building a new campus, a forty-million dollar physical plant to serve 10,000 plus students.

Realizing the advantages of having a continuous quality improvement process in place before moving to the new campus, the administration challenged Shelton State to implement Total Quality Management (TQM). As expected, College employees expressed mixed reactions, as well as uncertainty about change. When training sessions began with the train-the-trainer program, some of that uncertainty began to dissipate. The fifteen employees who took part in that initial training program were impressed with the concepts learned and began optimistically to spread their enthusiasm about the possibilities for applying TQM techniques to improve College operations. As faculty and staff began to realize that they, too, were going to receive training, even hard-core skeptics began to realize that TQM could possibly have a constructive impact on their jobs.

Faculty training has not been accomplished as quickly as hoped. However, it appears now that nearly all of the faculty will have completed training by the end of the fifth semester of employee training. Some faculty members have had difficulty scheduling training along with teaching loads, especially in technical and science teaching concentrations where contact and laboratory hours are extensive.

Shelton State named its continuous quality improvement program, TEAMSpirit. TEAMSpirit is an institutional plan to provide ongoing professional development training in TQM, to carry out the transition from a largely ineffective committee system in college governance to a team-based model, and to establish procedures that continuously improve the processes through which services are delivered to customers, both internal and external. This model is depicted in Table 25.

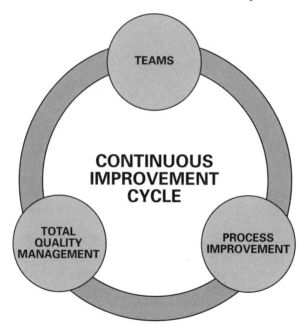

Table 25—Shelton State TEAMSpirit Professional Development Plan

Shelton State embraced a continuous improvement cycle consisting of three components: (1) training, (2) implementation of teams, and (3) process improvement. The restructuring of the college committee system to a team-based model is the organizational component of Shelton State's continuous improvement cycle. The team-based model is built around a cluster concept of grouping related core processes into *quality clusters*. Five quality clusters were identified. These include: (1) Educational Programs and Services, (2) External Programs and Community Relations, (3) Information Technology and Communications, (4) Administrative Systems and Services, and (5) Institutional Resources. They are graphically illustrated in Table 26.

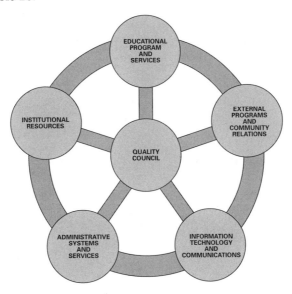

Table 26—Shelton State Five Quality Clusters

Teams are organized into one of four types of configurations as follows:

- Systems Improvement Team

- Process Improvement Team

- Delta Team

- Action Group

Responsibility for each quality cluster is assigned to a nine-member Systems Improvement (SI) Team. A key responsibility of each SI Team is to charter six-member Process Improvement (PI) teams to work on the improvement of selected processes. A formal chartering process ensures that processes being considered for improvement must meet pre-established selection criteria. Selection criteria include: customer impact, change potential, performance status, institutional impact, and resource impact. The chartering process protects the integrity of the team system by preventing the uncontrolled proliferation of teams. The Quality Council (QC) has developed a process by which the college's customers, both internal and external, can help the teams identify process improvement opportunities. To actively seek customer ideas and suggestions, the QC designed a simple, user-friendly form called a Process Improvement Form or PIF. An important part of this process is providing feedback to the customer on what action is undertaken. For customer feedback and internal tracking, the SI Team uses a PIF: Evaluation and Response Form. PIFs are routed to the appropriate Systems Improvement (SI) Team for evaluation and action. PIFs are scored and prioritized based on the evaluation criteria cited above. Then, Process Improvement (PI) Teams are chartered to work on the highest priority processes identified for improvement.

To add flexibility to the team model, a three-member Delta Team is used to *jump start* projects, react quickly to unexpected opportunities, and explore innovative approaches prior to formally chartering a Process Improvement Team. SI and PI Teams may also subdivide into Delta Teams for small-group work.

Shelton's Quality Council soon realized that the college needed more than system and process improvement teams; some mechanism was needed to carry on routine tasks separate from trying to improve their processes. Therefore, another kind of *team* was added to the TEAMSpirit blueprint; called Action Groups, they are responsible for dealing with routine and recurring tasks, functions, or activities at the college.

Team conversion began with a Delta Team comprised of the Director for Process Improvement, the Coordinator of Planning, and the head of the institution's TQM training process. This Delta Team began by collecting data, using TQM tools: (1) an interest survey of all personnel; (2) a minute paper about how people thought teams could work better than committees; and (3) cross-functional focus groups of faculty, staff, and administration that discussed the advantages of teams over committees. A special focus group of students discussed how students could or should serve on these teams. As a result, Shelton piloted several process improvement challenges and began to blueprint the transition from committees to teams. Because the process of transition has been approached methodically, speed of conversion has been deliberately conservative. All the people concerned want the process to be done correctly and are willing to expend the time necessary to use quality principles to carry out the transition.

Commitment to the principles of TQM differs among the various constituencies of the College. The administration is motivated by awareness that the College president and vice president are providing leadership to ensure that TQM becomes a reality at Shelton State to improve overall College services by sharing responsibilities with all employees. Some members of the administrative staff were already aware of the possibilities for improvement but were unfamiliar with the methodology of TQM. They were the first group to benefit from the services of the newly prepared train-the-trainers.

The next groups to be trained were members of the faculty and the support staff. Their enjoyment of the training sessions and their excited insights into the possibilities of empowerment and contribution became infectious. Morale improved but leveled off as few opportunities for application of training occurred. Determined not to lose the momentum of the staff's excitement, it was decided that the best approach to involve everybody on campus was to address more quickly the issue of shared college governance (required by the criteria of regional accrediting agencies).

The existing process was a cumbersome system of Standing College Committees. Because college policy required that all personnel be members of committees, membership on each committee was unmanageably large. Attendance at committee meetings was poor. If significant numbers did attend a meeting, the group was too large to effectively work on issues. If the group did manage to come up with some recommendations, communication breakdowns between committee and administration left them feeling ineffectual. Most Shelton employees would undoubtedly agree with Will Rogers who said, "Outside of traffic, there is nothing that has held this Country back as much as committees!"

Several approaches were used to tackle this problem. A brainstorming team was formed; faculty and staff were surveyed; a proposal was presented to and approved by the president, and announced to the College employees. The proposal attempted to deal with those issues that had the greatest potential for improving morale and, therefore, services. Instead of large, traditionally-run committees, the College would begin a transition toward small, self-managed teams. Because membership on teams would be limited to no more than 10 volunteers, not every employee was required to belong to a team every year. Some could elect to rotate out of service for a year or two. The team would share the responsibility of follow through on its proposals, rather than sending them to some administrator for implementation. These three aspects of the proposed shift to teams had an instant influence on the morale of the faculty and staff.

With TQM training, college personnel become excited about the opportunity to use some of the ideas and tools they had learned. They were also excited about being more involved in college governance and improving relationships between administrators, faculty, and support staff. Staff and faculty were particularly pleased about the prospect of not having to face the drudge of working on the old cumbersome committees, producing very little in the way of constructive ideas or actions. Morale began to improve, colored by cautious optimism about whether or not the team ideas would actually happen.

When an Implementation Design Team (IDT) was put together to develop a plan and a time line for shifting committees to teams, personnel were reassured about the real possibility of change. The IDT applied TQM principles and tools to the application of its business. Team members were enthusiastic about how much more work was accomplished during the meetings and how pleasant and satisfying team meetings became. As the SI teams were formed and the IDT announced them, along with its proceedings, in an institutional newsletter, faculty and staff interest intensified and morale was lifted again.

Of course, such profound changes take time and patience, and some doubt returned as the necessity for team training delayed team action. Throughout this process, small problem-solving teams have been formed to deal with immediate need issues. These teams have been cross functional, and their members report good experiences with getting to know and work with individuals from all areas of the College.

The impact of Continuous Quality Improvement at Shelton is evidenced in many ways. In the last year, the College hired a Director for Process Improvement, developed an implementation program for teamwork, adopted an institutional policy on continuous quality improvement, selected team members, and initiated ongoing team training by appointing a Director of Quality and Leadership Training.

Furthermore, the impact of the College's quality initiative has been reflected in the many local businesses which have come to Shelton to receive their own quality training. Even the local Chamber of Commerce requested that the College provide training for its staff. Truly there is evidence that quality is contagious.

Although training is not complete for all employees at the College, the culture of the College is being transformed. Meetings are more effective. The concept of *customers* is predominant in discussions of College policies. As instructors complete the TQM training course, they write *action plans* for implementing quality principles into their teaching. Many instructors now regularly include implementation of quality principles as a part of their professional development plans. An indicator of the effect of training is in some of these plans: "I plan to 'work toward becoming a facilitator in each of my classes rather than a disseminator,' 'I plan to make customers feel welcome and important.'"

Some of the instructors are utilizing the *tools of TQM* in their classes.

- One teacher in office management uses the affinity process on the first day of class to allow students to process their reasons for enrolling. She uses the results to plan units of instruction and to assist students in meeting their objectives.

- Another instructor in masonry has put each of the steps in his instruction on a flowchart so the instructor and the students are continually aware of the learning process.

- A library skills teacher uses the L-shaped matrix to examine the relationship between the required exercises in her class and the objectives that students are mastering in the course.

All of these are signs that instructors are actually using the information that is in the TQM training and that it is making a positive impact on the College.

Shelton State, however, is still in the early stages of TQM development. The sense of changing relationships among all facets of the institution and the improvement of morale and services comes chiefly from anecdotal information and some valuative data. Formal evaluation procedures are currently being developed through the team process. The College is currently working toward improving the percentage of personnel who have undergone TQM training. As the SI teams begin to work, some other training needs are emerging. It is an encouraging sign that the personnel involved in these first college teams are invested enough in the success of the process to request more information and training.

The impact of the quality initiative at Shelton State Community College has been most noticeable in the attitudes of the College employees. The culture of the College has undergone wholesale changes in the way it does business. Teachers now routinely gather to discuss the tools of quality that they employ in their classrooms. Support staff talk of innovative ways of better serving the students. The administration of the College meets regularly to discuss the transformation of the management culture to one of shared decision making.

Most of all, the College as a whole frequently asks the question, "Is this a quality way of serving our customers?" The College has developed an improved *attitude of quality*. TQM tools are being used to solve problems and people are beginning to reaffirm their involvement in the direction of the College because now they feel a sense of ownership.

At Shelton State Community College, quality is not a destination but a direction. This direction provides not only a more favorable work environment but also quality services for students who are, after all, the institution's reason for being.

Shelton State Community College

202 Skyland Boulevard

Skyland Campus

Tuscaloosa, AL 35405

Dr. Thomas E. Umphrey, President

Contact: Dr. Ted D. Spring, Vice President
Telephone: 205-391-2219

Western Iowa Tech
Community College

Western Iowa Tech Community College (WITCC) has been involved in Total Quality Management (TQM) for approximately five years. The process began with the selection of a vertical team which attended an introductory workshop on total quality techniques and quality transformation. That team has formed the core of the TQM steering team at the College. Adoption of TQM principles and processes has been an incremental, measured by a continuous growth in management converts and an accelerated level of commitment and involvement in total quality and institutional change. Much of the TQM's success is the result of the support and participation of Dr. Robert Dunker, President of the College.

The institution has seen TQM's positive potential in meeting major challenges such as unhappy customers, lack of resources, unmet needs, and employee morale. Notable areas of improvement include the processes for:

- Student orientation.

- Student advising.

- Staff development.

- Campus appearance and security.

Staff morale improved as a result of their participation in quality improvement teams. Staff have received training in team processes, problem-solving processes, strategies, and quality methods. Issues that teams address are identified not by top management, but at the staff level.

Other improvements were documented in a survey of students in 1995. The responses showed significant improvement in how students felt about campus security and comfort when compared to the benchmark 1990 responses.

Any major change such as TQM is likely to draw fire from cynics and skeptics. After about three years of work at the College, the results of team efforts proved to many that quality does make a difference. As a result, participation in the TQM movement has changed the College culture so that a significant number of staff are becoming process-oriented rather than event-oriented. Staff are beginning to think holistically and the outcomes of that change have reinforced positive attitudes toward TQM. This is consistent with research about TQM, that the road to quality is a process and not an event. In fact, it is not unusual for teams to produce results that differ surprisingly from original intent, yet these same recommendations are often creative, productive solutions to problems.

One of the most notable successes with the process improvement teams modified several different departments and their interrelationships. Those departments included: Central Receiving, the College Mailroom, Maintenance, Custodial, Grounds, and Security.

Two different process improvement teams set to work simultaneously to review mail delivery and the security system at the College. Through extensive research and review of processes and procedures, they determined that a major reorganization could save money, eliminate unneeded positions, and create a grounds crew which previously was an add-on to the maintenance and custodial staff. The team found that by reassigning custodial work, one full time Custodial position could be transferred to the Grounds Department. They also determined that by re-evaluating the security schedule, one full time Security position could be allocated to Grounds, and that by realigning the new College Mailroom with Central Receiving, an additional position could be transferred to the Grounds

Department. The outcome of this effort speaks for itself. No services were lost, several departments were realigned, internal and external customers were identified, and processes were developed for each of them to better serve our students.

In addition, the work of the quality teams was merged into the Strategic Plan. The issues identification, recommendations, and time frames contributed significantly to the Plan that was adopted in August, 1995.

Western Iowa Tech Community College

4647 Stone Avenue

PO Box 265

Sioux City, IA 51102-0265

Dr. Robert Dunker, President

Contact: Dr. Robert Dunker
Telephone: 712-274-6400

Chapter 8
Keeping the Quality
Momentum Going

Institutions involved in the quality improvement process for a long time know that it is important to put systems and processes in place to keep the quality momentum going. There are too many examples of organizations that have made progress with the quality initiative only to have something happen which changes things. A change in the top administration or the departure of one or more quality champions may turn things around drastically. Financial limitations also may create difficulties as there is the temptation to cut back some of the costs associated with the TQI effort when fiscal problems arise. These things may create problems and slow down the quality movement.

The major problem relates directly to the top leadership of the institution. All the experts agree that total quality improvement efforts require active and visible support and involvement by those in senior executive positions in the institution. Top managers become the beacons to make it all happen. A drastic shift in the styles and policies by individuals in key executive positions may have a negative impact across the institution. Special care is needed to avoid these shifts during personnel changes in key positions.

It's these lapses and changes in direction which have given TQI unfavorable publicity. Faculty and staff are somewhat used to the temporary nature of ideas and projects in education and are naturally skeptical about new things. They have seen it happen time and again. A new initiative is announced and everyone is geared up to move in a certain direction. Too often, these new ideas or projects are linked to federal or state initiatives. As the federal or state funds dry up, the emphasis changes to some other project. Soft money projects are so common in education that many people think short-term about most initiatives. It doesn't pay to announce that quality is a never-ending journey because faculty and staff have heard similar things before and they can't be blamed for being cautious. Other proactive measures are needed to gain lasting support.

A review of some experiences at educational institutions may be helpful as colleges consider whether TQI can be permanent. In one college, the profile used in the search for a new president was arrived at with active involvement by the faculty and staff. The position description had as its number one priority the requirement that the new president possess experience and knowledge about TQI in education. This profile was used in all the search announcements and the criteria appeared to offer the protection the faculty and staff wanted to ensure that the quality movement would remain an institutional priority.

Unfortunately, as candidates made application, several stated that they had considerable experience with TQI when, if fact, their exposure was limited. A few were able to convince the selection teams that they would be able to enhance the effort even though it was obvious their TQI backgrounds were not strong. The board of trustees made the final decision and selected someone with limited experiences in total quality improvement. The TQI initiative began to diminish after the new president arrived. Before long, the movement on campus all but disappeared.

In still another institution in the Midwest, the general morale of staff began to go down hill soon after a new president was appointed. The previous administration granted longer-term contracts to middle managers to reduce the fear that TQI typically brings to that tier of management. This job security assured them that while they were expected to change, their positions were not going to be eliminated. During his first two years, the new president terminated the contracts of three long-term managers and made several personnel changes including two demotions. The message to the institution was clear—people are expendable, especially at the mid-management level. Once again, fear spread throughout the campus.

In a large college in the Southwest, the dean of the school of technology was the quality champion for the organization. Several champions emerged as the faculty and staff participated in training. The initiative took hold and several solid quality-related projects produced outstanding results. The other deans began to notice these changes and some considered similar activities in their departments.

A new president arrived about this time and his agenda included massive reorganization. Before long, the dean of technology lost his power base and retired. Within a few months, the entire TQI process stalled and faculty became discouraged. Soon, things reverted to former ways.

In a fourth institution, a solid training philosophy existed and each staff member prepared a professional development plan. Resources were allocated to assist with that development. Each person also participated in intensive TQI training conducted by qualified on-site trainers. The programs were supported by top administration and everyone participated. As each new group began training, the president joined the class for a breakfast or lunch kick off. A hospitality budget was provided to make the sessions festive. Most of the staff looked forward to the training offered to all personnel including new employees.

When finances became limited, the new president decided that the TQI training should be voluntary. The hospitality budget was cut and the president rarely attended the kick off sessions. He generally sent a vice president or dean to greet the new groups and hand out the completion certificates. The faculty and staff noticed that the training priority had diminished and before long the quality momentum slowed.

While shifts in leadership styles should be expected and appreciated, the impact of these changes needs to be minimized as much as possible. People who have knowledge about TQI should be asked to help plan the strategy when major changes are expected. They should actively assist the selection teams in screening candidates for key positions to ensure that the top candidates have the quality experience so vital to keeping the momentum going. Involving the former president may be useful, especially in reviewing the TQI experiences of the candidate.

Changes in administration can be positive with the right individuals re-energizing the institution and revitalizing the TQI process. Selection of the right candidate with documented TQI experience will reassure everyone that TQI is permanent and will survive even with changes at the top.

In addition to changes in leadership there are other things which can stall the TQI momentum. One of these is to over-emphasize one facet of quality at the expense of others. Some quality experts put major emphasis into data collection, measurement, and accountability while ignoring the human resource features of quality. With this approach, staff look upon TQI as being an accountability program with primary emphasis on statistical approaches and control. Team development and decision making, customer service, organizational climate and cultural changes, and staff development and recognition programs are virtually ignored, and before long, the faculty and staff lose interest. TQI efforts will decline as the institution places too much emphasis on one aspect of the total quality initiative.

A lack of team facilitation is another reason why TQI efforts stall. Without support, teams are established in a haphazard way and the members are unsure of their roles and responsibilities. They try to learn team-building concepts and conflict resolution without any training. Without this vital resource, teams lose momentum, members get disheartened, and the teams lose their effectiveness.

Another example of quality failure relates to management support. Some managers fail to *walk their talk* even though they have been trained to know the language and skills of TQI. The faculty and staff have their expectations raised during training sessions and return to their departments to find their managers performing in the same old ways. Managers talk about quality quite a bit, but they just don't practice what they preach. The result is obvious. The momentum is slowed because visible leadership is lacking.

These kinds of mistakes happen because TQI requires major changes in how the organization operates. Strong leadership is critical to this paradigm shift and it is especially challenging when the management support and commitment is not present across the institution. Part of the problem relates to the past when management was expected to control and was rewarded accordingly. With TQI, managers are asked to give up a portion of their control and rely more on leadership skills and shared decision making. Mistakes are bound to occur because of the volume of change required. When they happen, it is best to admit that mistakes were made, if that seems feasible.

A new president can learn by communicating with customers and stakeholders before taking abrupt action. Getting to know students, faculty, staff, and people in the community takes patience and requires the president to spend time with people. The most important competency for a top administrator, therefore, is effective listening. This requires the leader to allow internal and external customers to define their needs and expectations before action is taken.

An example of an effective approach occurred in a Wisconsin college. The president set up a cross-functional team to study communication problems and recommend action to improve lines of communication across the college. The team did its job well and gathered information through a survey among all employees. A consultant was brought in to assist in the design of action plans for each strategy recommended. The president accepted the recommendations and the action plans were carried out. This approach was effective as it told the organization that the president was interested in being a listener and that he was willing to keep everyone informed.

The president also needs to set up systems to ensure that the board of trustees keeps out of administration and sticks to policy making. Board members often have pre-set ideas concerning what should be done and they try to influence the president and other top executives. A new administrator is especially vulnerable as many people seek to influence him/her. However, the motives of board members and key staff members may not necessarily be in the best interests of the organization. It is best for the new president to have patience and understanding and not make abrupt organizational changes. The best approach is to use the Plan-Do-Check-Act (PDCA) cycle as a planning vehicle right from the start.

SUMMARY COMMENTS

There are several danger points during TQI implementation. The quality movement is a long-term process and it requires top level support and commitment or several things may happen to slow the momentum. The following ideas may be useful to provide greater assurance that the TQI movement will remain secure:

1. When selecting a new chief administrator, use total quality improvement tools and techniques during the recruitment, selection, and orientation processes. Engage faculty and staff with experience as TQI facilitators to monitor the process.

2. Board members who are involved in the selection process of key executives need to understand the difference between talking about and actually practicing total quality improvement in education. New administrators who are selected for an institution involved in TQI, need strong, comprehensive TQI experience, or the momentum will soon stall.

3. TQI should remain a top priority, even during times of financial difficulty. Training and support for the team development process should be continued to ensure that the institution remains a *learning organization.*

4. Quality Improvement teams need guidance, support, and resources, especially in the start. The best approach is to have a group of trained facilitators available to assist teams as needed.

5. Administrators must be willing to *walk their talk*, and admit their mistakes.

6. New administrators should listen carefully to all stakeholders before making abrupt changes in the organization. All changes should follow the PDCA cycle.

7. Middle managers need special support and they should be given the security necessary to eliminate fear about their future in a TQI organization. The chief administrator should lead this effort and provide the resources needed to help people through this challenging period.

8. Education and training is necessary for all employees to ensure that they continue to understand and use the concepts, tools, and techniques of TQI. A *Learning Organization* philosophy puts priority on continued staff development.

9. Over-emphasis on measurement and accountability at the expenses of other TQI elements such as human development, customer service, team development, and communication will create problems with the quality movement.

Endnotes

1. Gleick, Elizabeth, "Privatized Lines," *Time* (Education), November 13, 1995.

2. "Educational Contracting in Trouble," *Time*, November, 13, 1995.

3. "Education Alternatives, Inc. Loses Baltimore Contract," <u>Wall Street Journal</u>, December 6, 1995, p. B4.

4. Nicholson, Roy A., "Re-Engineering the Way Education Does Business," (Presentation to National Noel-Levitz Conference) USA Group, Indianapolis, Indiana, July, 1995, p. 6.

5. Ibid., p. 20.

6. Willard R. Daggett, "Report Card on American Education" and "How to Raise the Grade," International Center for Leadership in Education, Schenectady, New York, 1993.

7. "Total Quality Management Survey Summary," Office of Graduate Studies and Research, Georgia Southern University, Statesboro, 1993.

8. Nicholson, Roy A., op.cit., "Re-Engineering the Way Education Does Business," USA Group, Indianapolis, Indiana, p. 4.

9. Spanbauer, Stanley J., *Making Quality Work in Education*, National Quality Academy, Appleton, Wisconsin, 1995.

10. Ibid.

11. Senge, Peter M., *The Fifth Discipline: The Art of Practice of the Learning Organization*, Doubleday, New York, 1990.

12. Op.cit., *Total Quality Management Survey Summary*, p. 4.

13. Carothers, Robert, "Quality on Campus: Good News from the Front," (Presentation at the National Institute for Quality Strategies in Education), 1993.

14. "Campus Trends," *American Council on Education*, 1993, and "Total Quality and Academic Practice," *Change*, May/June, 1993.

15. Anderson, Edward "Chip", UCLA Graduate School of Education (Presentation at the National Institute for Quality Strategies in Education), 1993.

16. Gross, Ronald, *Peak Learning*, GP Putman and Sons, New York, 1993.

17. Op.cit., *Peak Learning*, p. 78.

18. Roberts, Harry, "TQM in the Classroom," TQM Conference, Chicago, Illinois, April, 1993.

19. Angelo, T. A., Cross, K. P., *Classroom Assessment Techniques: A Handbook for College Teachers*, (2nd Edition), San Francisco, Jossey-Bass, 1993.

20. Roberts, Harry, op.cit., "TQM in the Classroom."

21. "Economic Development Guidelines," Fox Valley Technical College, Appleton, Wisconsin, 1984.

22. "Organizational Surveys," Rensis Likert Associates, Inc., Lansing, Michigan.

23. Mishler, Carol, "Analyzing Organizational Climate," Fox Valley Technical College, Appleton, Wisconsin, June, 1992.

24. Gentz, Merlin, "Annual Quality Report for Academic Affairs," Fox Valley Technical College, Appleton, Wisconsin, 1992-93.

25. "Fox Valley Technical College Foundation Annual Report," Haviland, Ruth, 1992-93.

26. "Administrative Services Annual Quality Report," Fox Valley Technical College, Martin, Robert F., 1992.

27. Op.cit., *Academic Affairs Annual Quality Report*, 1992.

28. "Using an Organizational Quality to Measure Progress Toward a Quality Culture—A Six-Year Effort," Mishler, Carol, Fox Valley Technical College, June, 1992.

29. Ibid.

Index

ALSO AVAILABLE FROM
USA GROUP NATIONAL QUALITY ACADEMY

Books

- A Quality System for Education, 1992
- Quality First in Education...Why Not?, 1990

Training Programs

- Quality Process Training for Service and Support Personnel
- Quality Training for Instructors
- Managing Customer Service
- Continuous Improvement Strategies in Education
- Making Quality Work in Education
- Team Building and Development
- Developing A TQI Plan for Your Campus
- Team Facilitator Training
- Effective Communication Strategies
- Connections™ (USA Group Noel-Levitz)
- Mastering Performance Reviews™ (USA Group Noel-Levitz)
- Partners™ (USA Group Noel-Levitz)
- Quality Process Training for Credit Union Personnel
- Quality—The Key to Expanding Credit Union Market Share
- Quality Process Training for Business and Industry Personnel
- Continuous Improvement Strategies
- Making Quality Work in Business, Industry, and Government

Assessment Tools

- Student Satisfaction Inventory™
- Campus Quality Survey™
- Credit Union Quality Survey™
- Member Satisfaction Survey™ (for Credit Unions)

Associate Degree Program

- Quality Improvement Process Specialist Degree Program
  - Quality as an Organizational Strategy
  - Customer Focus in Quality Improvement
  - Process Improvement
  - Internal and External Quality Standards
  - Project Management
  - Quality Improvement Process—Applied
  - Scientific Methods 1
  - Scientific Methods 2
  - Leadership for Quality

For Further Information

By phone: Please call between 8 a.m. and 4 p.m. Central Standard Time, Monday through Friday.
1-800-638-1202 or 414-730-6300

By fax: 414-730-1144

By mail: USA Group National Quality Academy
N615 Communication Drive, Suite 2A
Appleton, WI 54915

By e-mail: info@usanqa.com